ADVANCED LEVEL Six-Way Paragraphs

100 Passages for Developing
the Six Essential Categories of Comprehension

6

THIRD EDITION

WALTER PAUK

JAMESTOWN  PUBLISHERS

a division of NTC/CONTEMPORARY PUBLISHING GROUP
Lincolnwood, Illinois USA

Readability

Passages 1–20: Level H

Passages 21–40: Level I

Passages 41–60: Level J

Passages 61–80: Level K

Passages 81–100: Level L

ISBN (introductory level): 0-8442-2124-4
ISBN (middle level): 0-8442-2119-8
ISBN (advanced level): 0-8442-2123-6

Published by Jamestown Publishers,
a division of NTC/Contemporary Publishing Group, Inc.,
4255 West Touhy Avenue,
Lincolnwood (Chicago), Illinois 60712-1975 U.S.A.

00 01 02 03 04 VL 10 9 8 7 6 5 4 3

Contents

The Paragraph

The paragraph! That's the working unit of both writer and reader. The writer works hard to put meaning into the paragraph; the reader works hard to take meaning out of it. Though they work at opposite tasks, the work of each is closely related. Actually, to understand better the job of the reader, one must first understand better the job of the writer. So, let us look briefly at the writer's job.

One Main Idea. To make their meaning clear, writers know that they must follow certain basic principles. First, they know that they must develop only one main idea per paragraph. This principle is so important that they know it backward too. They know that they must not try to develop two main ideas in the same paragraph.

The Topic Sentence. The next important principle they know is that each main idea can be stated in a topic sentence, and that such a sentence best serves its function by coming at or near the beginning of its paragraph. They know too, that the more clearly they can state the topic of a paragraph in the opening sentence, the more effective they will be in developing a meaningful, well-organized paragraph.

One word of warning to the reader: There is no guarantee that the topic sentence will always be the first sentence of a paragraph. Occasionally, a writer will start off with an introductory or a transitional sentence. Then, it is up to the reader to spot such a sentence and recognize it for what it is.

The topic sentence may be placed in several other positions in a paragraph. It may be placed in the middle, or even at the very end. If it appears at the end, though it may still be a topic sentence in form, in terms of function, it is more rightfully a *restatement*. Whenever the end position is chosen, it is chosen to give the restatement especial emphasis.

Finally, a paragraph may not have a topic sentence in it at all. Some writers purposely leave out such sentences. But, in such cases, inferring a topic sentence may not be as difficult as it may first appear. Here's why. Many such professional writers actually do write topic sentences, but on separate scraps of paper. They then place one of the scraps at the head of a sheet and use the topic sentence to guide their thoughts in the construction of the paragraph. With the paragraph written and the topic sentence having served its purpose, the scrap is discarded. The end result is a paragraph without a visible topic sentence, but the paragraph, nonetheless, has embedded in it all the clues that an alert reader needs for making an accurate inference.

Finding Meaning. Actually, there is nothing especially important in recognizing or inferring a topic sentence for its own sake. The important thing is that the reader use the topic sentence as a quick means of establishing a focal point around which to cluster the meanings of the subsequent words and sentences that he or she reads. Here's the double-edged sword again: just as writers use topic sentences to provide focus and structure for presenting their meaning, so the perceptive reader can use the topic sentence for focus and structure to gain meaning.

Up to this point, the reader, having looked secretly over the writer's shoulder, should have learned two exceedingly valuable secrets: first, expect only one main idea in each paragraph; and secondly, use the topic sentence to discover the topic of each paragraph.

Supporting the Main Idea. Now, there is more to a writer's job than writing paragraphs that consist of only bare topic sentences and main ideas. The balance of the job deals with developing each main idea through the use of supporting material that amplifies and clarifies the main idea and, many times, makes it more vivid and memorable.

To support their main ideas, writers may use a variety of forms. One of the most common is the example. Examples help to illustrate the main idea. Other supporting materials are anecdotes, incidents, jokes, allusions, comparisons, contrasts, analogies, definitions, exceptions, logic, and so forth.

To summarize, the reader should have learned from the writer that a textbook-type paragraph usually contains these three elements: a topic sentence, a main idea, and supporting material. Knowing this, the reader should use the topic sentence to find the main idea. Everything other than the main idea is supporting material used to illustrate, amplify, and qualify the main idea. So the reader must be able to separate the main idea from the supporting material, yet see the relationship between them.

To the Student

The Six Types of Questions

In this book, the basic skills necessary for reading factual material are taught through the use of the following six types of questions: subject matter, main idea, supporting details, conclusion, clarifying devices, and vocabulary in context questions.

Subject Matter. This question looks easy and often is easy. But don't let that fool you into thinking it isn't important. The subject matter question can help you with the most important skill of all reading and learning: concentration. With it, you comprehend and learn. Without it, you fail.

Here is the secret for gaining concentration: After reading the first few lines of something, ask yourself, "What is the subject matter of this passage?" Instantly, you will be thinking about the passage. You will be concentrating. If you don't ask this question, your eyes will move across the lines of print, yet your mind will be thinking of other things.

By asking this question as you read each passage in this book, you will master the skill so well that it will carry over to everything you read.

Let's see how this method works. Here is a short passage:

> Do you want to be a good speaker? If so, then think before you speak, and think while you speak. Take care to pronounce words well. Do not speak your words too hastily. Use words your audience can understand. Do not speak in the same tone all the time. Cut out all mannerisms such as making the same gesture over and over again. Do not point or jab your finger at the audience. And don't forget to use your voice to express your feelings.

On finishing the first sentence your thought should have been something like, "Ah, a passage on speaking. Maybe I can pick up a few good tips." If it was, your head was in the right place. By focusing right away on the subject matter, you'll be concentrating, you'll be looking for something, your attitude will be superb, and best of all, you'll be understanding, learning, and remembering.

Main Idea. In reading anything, once you have grasped the subject matter, ask yourself, "What point is the writer trying to make?" Once you ask this question, your mind will be looking for an answer, and chances are that you will find one. But if you don't focus in this way, all things seem equal. Nothing stands out.

Try to find the main idea in the following passage by asking, "What point is the writer trying to make?"

> A horseshoe means good luck. This is true in every country. The good luck comes partly because the shoe is made of iron, and also because its shape is like a crescent moon. It is very good luck to find a horseshoe by the side of the road. It is extra good luck if the shoe was thrown from the right rear leg of a grey mare. Horseshoes are usually hung over the outside doorways of houses.

A good answer is, "Horseshoes mean good luck." This passage is fairly easy to figure out because the first sentence is an excellent topic sentence.

The next example does not have a topic sentence. Nevertheless, the question "What point is the writer trying to make?" can still be answered. This time, think about the passage and come up with your own answer.

> What will the newborn baby be like when it grows up? Friends and parents would like to know. Some people believe you can find out by placing a coin in the child's right hand. If the baby holds the coin tightly, it means that the child will grow up to save money. If it is held loosely, it means the baby will be generous. If the coin is dropped, the child will be a spender.

This passage may have required a bit more thought, for the correct answer is a summary type answer. Compare your answer with the following main idea statement: "Some people use a coin to try to find out a baby's future."

Supporting Details. In common usage, the word *detail* has taken on the unrespected meaning of "something relatively unimportant." But details are important. Details are the plaster, board, and brick of a building, while main ideas are the large, strong steel or wooden beams. A solid, well-written passage must contain both.

The bulk of a factual passage is made up of details that support the main idea. The main idea is often buried among the details. You have to dig to distinguish between them. Here are some characteristics that can help you see the difference between supporting details and main ideas.

First, supporting details come in various forms, such as examples, explanations, descriptions, definitions, comparisons, contrasts, exceptions, analogies, similes, and metaphors.

Second, these various kinds of details are used to support the main idea. The words themselves, supporting details, spell out their job. So when you have trouble finding the main idea, take a passage apart sentence by sentence, asking, "Does this sentence support something, or is this the thing being supported?" In other words, you must not only separate the two, but also see how they help one another. The main idea can often be expressed in a single sentence. But a sentence cannot tell a complete story. The writer must use additional sentences to give you the full picture.

The following passage shows how important details are for providing a full picture of what the writer had in mind.

> This book has provided us with a marvelous record of village life in the mountains of Lebanon 100 years ago. In one picture, we see women baking bread in clay ovens, their children looking on hungrily. On the next page there is a man dancing with a jar on his head at a village feast. Another sketch shows two women sitting on a rug chopping vegetables. In another drawing, a man is drinking from a clay jug. The water in the jug travels in a perfect arc from the spout to his mouth. In the villages people still drink water in this way.

Here we have the main idea in one sentence—the first sentence. Having stated the main idea, the writer goes on to give example after example of the "marvelous record." These examples are supporting details.

Conclusion. As a reader moves through a passage, grasping the main idea and supporting details, it is natural for him or her to begin to guess an ending or conclusion. Some passages contain conclusions. Others do not. It all depends on the writer's purpose. For example, some passages describe a process—how something is done. There is no sense in trying to draw a conclusion from such a passage.

There are two kinds of passages with conclusions. In one, the conclusion is stated by the author. In the other, the conclusion is merely implied by the author. That is, the author seems to have come to a conclusion, but has not stated it. It is up to you to draw that conclusion.

Look for the conclusion that is stated in the following passage.

> A thunderstorm in the desert can bring surprises. Put yourself in this situation. A thunderstorm roars up in the distance to cool off your sun-baked car, and you head toward it, hoping for a few cool moments. You see the huge black cloud, the flashes of lightning, the black sheets of rain falling. Finally you are under the cloudburst, but you aren't getting rained on. Not a drop reaches your car. You stop the car, get out, and look up. There, right above you, is the storm. Rain is pouring down toward you, but every bit of it evaporates before it gets close enough to wet you.

The conclusion to this passage is that though it rains above the desert, the rain doesn't reach the ground because it is evaporated by the hot, dry air.

In the next excerpt, the author strongly implies a conclusion, but does not state it directly.

> In fact, what I've said adds up to this: if you wish to enjoy your holiday in the Middle East, I suggest that you simply make up your mind that although you can get your money's worth if you're careful, and can make excellent purchases if you take your time, there are few bargains to be had. This is true of carpets, anyway.

From the excerpt above, we can draw the conclusion that carpets cannot be bought cheaply in the Middle East.

Looking for a conclusion puts you in the shoes of a detective. While reading, you have to think, "Where is the writer leading me? What's the conclusion?" And, like a detective, you must try to guess the conclusion, changing the guess as you get more and more information.

Clarifying Devices. Clarifying devices are words, phrases, and techniques that a writer uses to make main ideas, sub-ideas, and supporting details clear and interesting. By knowing some of these clarifying and controlling devices, you will be better able to recognize them in the passages you read. By recognizing them, you will be able to read with greater comprehension and speed.

Two literary devices that make a writer's ideas both clear and interesting are similes and metaphors. Both are used to make comparisons that add color and power to ideas. An example of a simile is "She has a mind like a computer." In this simile, a person's mind is compared to a computer. A simile always uses the words *like, as,* or *than* to make a comparison. The metaphor, on the other hand, makes a direct comparison: "Her mind is a computer." Because metaphors are shorter and more direct, they are more forceful than similes. Writers use them to capture your attention, touch your emotions, and spark your imagination.

The largest single group of clarifying devices, and the most widely used, are transitional or signal words. For example, here are some signal words that you see all the time: *first, second, next, last, finally.* A writer uses such words to keep ideas, steps in a process, or lists in order. Other transitional words include *in brief, in conclusion, above all, therefore, since, because,* and *consequently.*

Organizational patterns are also clarifying devices. One such pattern is the chronological pattern, in which events unfold in the order of time: one thing happens first, then another, and another, and so on. A time pattern orders events. The event may take place in five minutes or over a period of hundreds of years.

Vocabulary in Context. How accurate are you in using words you think you already know? Do you know that the word *exotic* means "a thing or person from a foreign country?" So, exotic flowers and exotic dancers are flowers and dancers from a foreign country. Exotic has been used incorrectly so often and for so long that it has developed a second meaning. Most people use exotic to mean "strikingly unusual, as in color or design."

Many people think that the words *imply* and *infer* mean the same thing. They do not. An author may imply, or suggest, something. The reader then infers what the author implied. In other words, to imply is to suggest an idea. To infer is to take meaning out.

It would be easy to see what would happen to a passage if a reader skipped a word or two that he or she did not know, and imposed fuzzy meanings on a few others. The result would inevitably be a gross misunderstanding of the author's message. You will become a better reader if you learn the exact meanings and different shades of meaning of the words that are already familiar to you.

Answering the Main Idea Question

The main idea questions in this book are not the usual multiple-choice variety from which you must select the one correct statement. Rather, you are given three statements and are asked to select the statement that expresses the main idea of the passage, the statement that is too narrow, and the statement that is too broad. You have to work hard and actively to identify all three statements correctly. This new type of question teaches you the differences among statements that, at first, seem almost equal.

To help you handle these questions, let's go behind the scenes to see how the main idea questions in this book were constructed. The true main idea statement was always written first. It had to be neat, succinct, and positive. The main idea tells who or what the subject of the passage is. It also answers the question does what? or is what? Next, keeping the main idea statement in mind, the other two statements were written. They are variations of the main idea statement. The too narrow statement had to be in line with the main idea, but express only part of it. Likewise, the too broad statement had to be in line with the main idea, but to be too general in scope.

Read the sample passage that starts below. Then, to learn how to answer the main idea questions, follow the instructions in the box. The answer to each part of the question has been filled in for you. The score for each answer has also been marked.

Sample Passage

   Did you know you can predict weather by watching swallows? When swallows fly high, you can expect fine weather. But when they fly low, or close to the ground, rain is on the way. Swallows follow flies and gnats, which delight in warm currents of air. Warm air is lighter than cold air, and when the warm air currents are high in the sky, then there is less of a chance of rain. When the warm air is near the ground, then it is certain there will be rain.

Main Idea   1

	Answer	Score
Mark the *main idea*	M	15
Mark the statement that is *too broad*	B	5
Mark the statement that is *too narrow*	N	5

a. By watching swallows, a person can predict rain or fair weather.   **M**   15

[This statement gathers all the important points. It gives a correct picture of the main idea in a brief way: (1) watching swallows, (2) predicting rain, and (3) predicting fair weather.]

b. When swallows fly high, there is less chance of rain.   **B**   5

[This statement is correct, but it is too narrow. Only part of the main idea is stated. The prediction for rain is left out.]

c. People can predict weather by watching birds in flight.   **N**   5

[This statement is too broad. It is stretching the point by saying "by watching birds in flight." According to the passage, only one kind of bird, swallows, can let us know whether or not it will rain.]

Getting the Most Out of This Book

The following steps could be called "tricks of the trade." Your teachers might call them "rules for learning." It doesn't matter what they are called. What does matter is that they work.

Think About the Title. A famous language expert told me a "trick" to use when I read. "The first thing to do is to read the title. Then spend a few moments thinking about it."

Writers spend much time thinking up good titles. They try to pack a lot of meaning into them. It makes sense, then, for you to spend a few seconds trying to dig out some meaning. These few moments of thought will give you a head start on a passage.

Thinking about the title can help you in another way, too. It helps you concentrate on a passage before you begin reading. Why does this happen? Thinking about the title fills your head full of thoughts about the passage. There's no room for anything else to get in to break concentration.

The Dot System. Here is a method that will speed up your reading. It also builds comprehension at the same time.

Spend a few moments with the title. Then read quickly through the passage. Next, without looking back, answer the six questions by placing a dot in the box next to each answer of your choice. The dots will be your "unofficial" answers. For the main idea question (question one) place your dot in the box next to the statement that you think is the main idea.

The dot system helps by making you think hard on your first, fast reading. The practice you gain by trying to grasp and remember ideas makes you a stronger reader.

The Check-Mark System. First, answer the main idea question. Follow the steps that are given above each set of statements for this question. Use a capital letter to mark your final answer to each part of the main idea question.

You have answered the other five questions with a dot. Now read the passage once more carefully. This time, mark your final answer to each question by placing a check mark (✓) in the box next to the answer of your choice. The answers with the check marks are the ones that will count toward your score.

The Diagnostic Chart. Now move your final answers to the Diagnostic Chart that starts on page 209.

Use the row of boxes beside Passage 1 for the answers to the first passage. Use the row of boxes beside Passage 2 for the answers to the second passage, and so on. Write the letter of your answer to the left of the dotted line in each block.

Correct your answers using the Answer Key on pages 203–207. When scoring your answers, do not use an x for incorrect or a c for correct. Instead, use this method. If your choice is incorrect, write the letter of the correct answer to the right of the dotted line in the block.

Thus, the row of answers for each passage will show your incorrect answers. And it will also show the correct answers.

Your Total Comprehension Score. Go back to the passage you have just read. If you answered a question incorrectly, draw a line under the correct choice on the question page. Then write your score for each question on the line provided. Add the scores to get your total comprehension score. Enter that number in the box marked Total Score.

Graphing Your Progress. After you have found your total comprehension score, turn to the Progress Graph that begins on page 215. Write your score in the box under the number of the passage. Then put an *x* along the line above the box to show your total comprehension score. Join the *x*'s as you go. This will plot a line showing your progress.

Taking Corrective Action. Your incorrect answers give you a way to teach yourself how to read better. Take the time to study your wrong answers.

Go back to the questions. For each question you got wrong, read the correct answer (the one you have underlined) several times. With the correct answer in mind, go back to the passage itself. Read to see why the approved answer is better. Try to see where you made your mistake. Try to figure out why you chose a wrong answer.

The Steps in a Nutshell

Here's a quick review of the steps to follow. Following these steps is the way to get the most out of this book. Be sure you have read and understood everything in the "To the Student" section on pages ix–xvii before you start.

1. **Think About the Title of the Passage.** Try to get all the meaning the writer put into it.
2. **Read the Passage Quickly.**
3. **Answer the Questions, Using the Dot System.** Use dots to mark your unofficial answers. Don't look back at the passage.
4. **Read the Passage Again—Carefully.**
5. **Mark Your Final Answers.** Put a check mark (✔) in the box to note your final answer. Use capital letters for each part of the main idea question.

6. **Mark Your Answers on the Diagnostic Chart.** Record your final answers on the Diagnostic Chart that begins on page 209. Write your answers to the left of the dotted line in the answer blocks for the passage.

7. **Correct Your Answers.** Use the Answer Key on pages 203–207. If an answer is not correct, write the correct answer in the right side of the block, beside your wrong answer. Then go back to the question page. Place a line under the correct answer.

8. **Find Your Total Comprehension Score.** Find this by adding up the points you earned for each question. Enter the total in the box marked Total Score.

9. **Graph Your Progress.** Enter and plot your score on the graph that begins on page 215.

10. **Take Corrective Action.** Read your wrong answers. Read the passage once more. Try to figure out why you were wrong.

To the Instructor

The Reading Passages
Each of the 100 passages included in the book had to meet the following three criteria: high interest level, appropriate readability level, and factual content.

The high interest level was assured by choosing passages of mature content that would appeal to a wide range of readers.

The passages in *Six-Way Paragraphs, Introductory Level* range from reading level 1 through reading level 4, with 25 passages on each level. *Six-Way Paragraphs, Middle Level* contains passages that range from reading level 4 to reading level 8, with 20 passages on each reading level. The passages in *Six-Way Paragraphs, Advanced Level* range from reading level 8 to reading level 12, with 20 passages on each reading level.

The factual content was a definite requirement because by reading factual passages students build not only their reading skills but, of equal importance, their informational backgrounds.

The Six Questions
This book is organized around six essential questions. The most important of these is the main idea question, which is actually a set of three statements. Students must first choose and label the statement that expresses the main idea of the passage; then they must label each of the other statements as being either too narrow or too broad to be the main idea.

In addition to the main idea question, there are five other questions. These questions are within the framework of the following five categories: subject matter, supporting details, conclusions, clarifying devices, and vocabulary in context.

By repeated practice with the questions within these six categories, students will develop an active, searching attitude that will carry over to the reading of other expository prose. These six types of questions will help them become aware of what they are reading at the time they are actually seeing the words and phrases on a page. This type of thinking-while-reading sets the stage for higher comprehension and better retention.

The Diagnostic Chart
The Diagnostic Chart provides the most dignified form of guidance yet devised. With this chart, no one has to point out a student's weaknesses. The chart does that

automatically, yielding the information directly and personally to the student, making self-teaching possible. The organization of the questions and the format for marking answers on the chart are what make it work so well.

The six questions for each passage are always in the same order. For example, the question designed to teach the skill of drawing conclusions is always the fourth question, and the main idea question is always first. Keeping the questions in a set order sets the stage for the smooth working of the chart.

The chart works automatically when students write the letter of their answer choices for each passage in the spaces provided. Even after completing only one passage, the chart will reveal the type or types of questions answered correctly, as well as the types answered incorrectly. As the answers for more passages are recorded, the chart will show the types of questions that are missed consistently. A pattern can be seen after three or more passages have been completed. For example, if a student answers question 4 (drawing conclusions) incorrectly for three out of four passages, the student's weakness in this area shows up automatically.

Once a weakness is revealed, have your students take the following steps: First, turn to the instructional pages in the beginning of the book, and study the section in which the topic is discussed. Second, go back and reread the questions that were missed in that particular category. Then, with the correct answer to a question in mind, read the entire passage again, trying to see how the author developed the answer to the question. Do this for each question that was missed. Third, when reading future passages, make an extra effort to correctly answer the questions in that particular category. Fourth, if the difficulty continues, arrange to see the instructor.

ADVANCED LEVEL Six-Way Paragraphs

1 Tulipmania

It's a simple law of business: if an item is scarce and many people want it, the price goes up. It happens with certain kinds of toys during the holiday season. It happens with tickets to important sports events. But could you imagine it happening to the price of tulips?

Tulips weren't always grown in Holland; the first bulbs were transported there from the Turkish Empire in 1593. But the botanist who brought them into the country was very stingy with them, refusing to give them away or even sell them. People gradually got their hands on the bulbs, but they remained a rarity that only the rich could afford.

Tulips were so bright and beautiful that many people desired them. And so the price kept escalating. The most popular tulips of all had alternating broken stripes of two different colors. These so-called bizarre patterns, which were actually caused by a tulip virus, meant that every single tulip had a unique look. So prized were such tulips that in 1624 certain varieties of them were selling for $1,500 a bulb! A short time later that price had skyrocketed to $2,250.

Between 1634 and 1637 the market for bi-color tulips went completely berserk. Not only the rich but trade and craft people as well were furiously bidding up prices, sometimes paying for one bulb the equivalent of what it would cost to feed and clothe a small town. In fact, the highest price ever recorded for a bulb was over $400,000.

And then, as you might expect, the market collapsed. Just as in the stock market crash of 1929, many people were financially ruined. But amid the <u>lamentations</u>, despair, and suicides, the modest tulip continued to beautify the Dutch countryside.

Main Idea 1

	Answer	Score
Mark the *main idea*	M	15
Mark the statement that is *too broad*	B	5
Mark the statement that is *too narrow*	N	5

a. The price for tulip bulbs rose extravagantly and then fell sharply in the early 1600s. ☐ ____

b. Some tulip bulbs sold for over $2,000 apiece. ☐ ____

c. Prices will rise on anything that is scarce and desirable. ☐ ____

Subject Matter   **2**   The most appropriate alternate title for this passage would be
☐ a. The Rise and Fall of the Tulip Market.
☐ b. Beautiful and Colorful.
☐ c. Holland's Prize Flower.
☐ d. A Gift from the Turks.   _____

Supporting Details   **3**   The most desirable tulips were
☐ a. red.
☐ b. pink.
☐ c. white.
☐ d. bi-colored.   _____

Conclusion   **4**   With "bizarre" tulips, people
☐ a. could not predict what a new bulb would look like.
☐ b. often planted hundreds in their gardens.
☐ c. handed the bulbs down to their grandchildren.
☐ d. sometimes became ill from the virus themselves.   _____

Clarifying Devices   **5**   The author of this passage refers to the 1929 stock market crash in order to
☐ a. make the tulip story sound more modern.
☐ b. point out its similarity to the fall of the tulip market.
☐ c. show that people from every century are greedy.
☐ d. emphasize the value of good investments.   _____

Vocabulary in Context   **6**   Lamentations means
☐ a. uncertainty.
☐ b. songs of joy.
☐ c. buying.
☐ d. cries of sorrow.   _____

Add your scores for questions 1–6. Enter the total here and on the graph on page 215.   **Total Score**   _____

3

2 Crack Shot

Outside the castle, the grim ritual was enacted yet again. A solitary man strolled across the field, his ragged clothing indicating his peasant status. The king appeared in the window, raised his rifle to his shoulder, and took careful aim; at the crack of gunfire, the solitary figure crumpled noiselessly to the dirt of the courtyard. A short while later, the body would be carried off. The king turned away from the window, strangely satisfied that he could rest in peace another day.

Otto of Bavaria had <u>succeeded</u> to the throne in 1886, but he never actually ruled his kingdom. For most of his life he was confined to his room, where he held conversations with the ghosts that lived in his dresser drawer. His family kept him from the exercise of his kingly powers, but the voices he heard in his room urged him to commit awful deeds. Each day, to ensure his well being and his peace of mind, one peasant had to die at his hands. So every day outside his bedroom window the gruesome scene was repeated.

Each day the guards carefully loaded the king's gun with blanks, and each day a soldier dressed in rags would walk outside the castle and fall when the king fired his gun. In this way, the king's family humored his illness; the mad king went to his grave convinced that he had killed hundreds of innocent people.

Main Idea 1

	Answer	Score
Mark the _main idea_	M	15
Mark the statement that is _too broad_	B	5
Mark the statement that is _too narrow_	N	5

a. To satisfy his strange desire, mad King Otto's family deluded him by making him think that he had killed the peasants. ☐ _____

b. Throughout history, royalty have been humored in their desires. ☐ _____

c. A soldier dressed in rags pretended to fall when shot at. ☐ _____

Score 15 points for each correct answer.   **Score**

Subject Matter   **2**   This passage is mostly about
- ☐ a. the decline of European royalty.
- ☐ b. the care of invalids.
- ☐ c. King Otto's madness.
- ☐ d. military service.   _____

Supporting Details   **3**   Otto was kept from exercising authority by
- ☐ a. parliament.
- ☐ b. the judges.
- ☐ c. leaders of the army.
- ☐ d. his family.   _____

Conclusion   **4**   It is believable that Otto could get away with shooting peasants because kings once
- ☐ a. ruled large territories.
- ☐ b. had the power of life and death over their subjects.
- ☐ c. were the wealthiest in their kingdom.
- ☐ d. passed the throne to their eldest sons.   _____

Clarifying Devices   **5**   The author of this passage develops suspense by
- ☐ a. not disclosing the deception until the end.
- ☐ b. emphasizing the family's role.
- ☐ c. generalizing about monarchies.
- ☐ d. listing the king's unsavory characteristics.   _____

Vocabulary in Context   **6**   The word <u>succeeded</u> as used in this passage means
- ☐ a. declined.
- ☐ b. inherited.
- ☐ c. financed.
- ☐ d. won.   _____

Add your scores for questions 1–6. Enter the total here and on the graph on page 215.   **Total Score**   _____

5

3 Keeping a Promise

The movie *Butch Cassidy and the Sundance Kid* portrayed outlaw Butch Cassidy as a charming and <u>sympathetic</u> fellow. Apparently, the movie's portrayal of Cassidy was remarkably true to life. The robberies that Cassidy's gang, the Wild Bunch, committed often had a Robin Hood quality; that is, they did not rob the poor but only the rich.

Butch himself never killed anyone. His only known gunfight took place in Bolivia. He was killed in it. He preferred to surprise and awe rather than to kill or hurt. Nevertheless, he was, in fact, fast and accurate with a gun. He could fast-draw and hit a playing card nailed to a distant tree or shatter a bottle tossed into the air.

Stories about Butch reveal his unusual charm and personal honesty, which remained intact even as he went about committing robberies. For instance, the only time Butch was ever captured and convicted, he talked his jailers into allowing him to go out on the town before being locked up. He came back the next day as promised.

After a year in jail, Cassidy's charm once again helped him. He was set free by the governor of Wyoming after promising to leave Wyoming's cattle and banks alone. Butch again kept his promise. It is true that he never held up any banks or ran off with any cattle in Wyoming, but he started holding up and robbing the railroads in Wyoming, for railroads weren't mentioned in the agreement with the governor.

Main Idea	1		
		Answer	**Score**
	Mark the *main idea*	M	15
	Mark the statement that is *too broad*	B	5
	Mark the statement that is *too narrow*	N	5

a. The Wild Bunch was like Robin Hood's gang. ☐ N ____

b. Butch Cassidy was a charming outlaw who always kept his word. ☐ M ____

c. Many crimes were committed in the Old West. ☐ B ____

Subject Matter   **2**   This passage is mostly about
  - ☐ a. the governor of Wyoming.
  - ☐ b. the movie *Butch Cassidy and the Sundance Kid.*
  - ☑ c. Butch Cassidy.
  - ☐ d. jailers of the Old West.   _____

Supporting Details   **3**   Why did the jailers let Butch out?
  - ☐ a. They were not well trained.
  - ☐ b. They were old friends of Butch.
  - ☑ c. Butch talked them into it.
  - ☐ d. They knew Butch was not guilty.   _____

Conclusion   **4**   Cassidy's shooting skill can be described as
  - ☐ a. below average.
  - ☐ b. inconvenient.
  - ☑ c. accurate.
  - ☐ d. deadly.   _____

Clarifying Devices   **5**   The author develops the main idea by
  - ☑ a. comparing the movie with Butch's real life.
  - ☐ b. telling stories about Butch.
  - ☐ c. recalling people's descriptions of Butch.
  - ☐ d. setting forth damaging evidence.   _____

Vocabulary in Context   **6**   <u>Sympathetic</u> is used to mean
  - ☐ a. sorrowful.
  - ☑ b. talkative.
  - ☐ c. likable.
  - ☐ d. two-faced   _____

**Add your scores for questions 1–6. Enter the total here
and on the graph on page 215.**   **Total
Score**   _____

7

4 Acrobatic Worms

When a moth or butterfly first hatches from the egg, it is in the wormlike larva stage. After a period of development, the larva spins a cocoon, and eventually a full-grown moth or butterfly emerges. But who has ever heard of a moth emerging from a vegetable seed?

There is a kind of moth that emerges from the Mexican jumping bean. The bean is actually a seed that grows on a shrub resembling the rubber tree. The flowers of this shrub are put to a very unusual use. Huge swarms of moths, thick as clouds, hover over the blossoms and deposit their eggs among the petals. After a while, the eggs hatch into tiny caterpillars, which bore into the hollow seeds of the plant. Once inside, the larvae survive by slowly eating the walls of their new homes—the inner tissue of the seeds!

When the worms chew the walls or wriggle inside the beans, the Mexican jumping beans begin to roll and hop. The larvae must stay away from direct sunlight, or the beans' centers become dangerously hot. So, when sun shines on a bean, the larva begins jumping inside until the bean rolls to a shady spot. The warmer it gets, the faster the bean rolls and hops.

The exact distance that a bean can jump has not been measured, but people who have watched these beans jump say it is quite impressive. Considering its size, the tiny larva is a powerful athlete.

Main Idea   1

	Answer	Score
Mark the *main idea*	M	15
Mark the statement that is *too broad*	B	5
Mark the statement that is *too narrow*	N	5

a. Mexican jumping beans jump because tiny caterpillars inside them jump around. ☐ _____

b. Tiny moth caterpillars live inside the Mexican jumping beans. ☐ _____

c. The Mexican jumping bean is an intriguing seed. ☐ _____

Subject Matter　2　Another good title for this story might be
- [ ] a. The Mexican Jumping Bean.
- [ ] b. The Mystery of Hollow Seeds.
- [ ] c. A Cozy Home.
- [ ] d. Too Hot to Handle.

_____

Supporting Details　3　The jumping bean hops faster when
- [ ] a. people watch.
- [ ] b. the larva is hungry.
- [ ] c. the sun shines on it.
- [ ] d. it's raining.

_____

Conclusion　4　How far a bean can jump remains a mystery because
- [ ] a. people think it's magic.
- [ ] b. people don't understand the bean.
- [ ] c. the bean doesn't hop, it merely rolls.
- [ ] d. no one has measured the distance.

_____

Clarifying Devices　5　In the third sentence, the author creates interest by
- [ ] a. stating a scientific fact.
- [ ] b. asking a surprising question.
- [ ] c. warning the reader.
- [ ] d. appealing to the reader's sense of humor.

_____

Vocabulary in Context　6　The word <u>considering</u> is closest in meaning to
- [ ] a. with the help of.
- [ ] b. knowing.
- [ ] c. taking into account.
- [ ] d. watching.

_____

Add your scores for questions 1–6. Enter the total here and on the graph on page 215.　　**Total Score**

_____

5 The Century Flower

Imagine a plant that blooms only once every hundred years. What wonders might that century bring? During the last hundred years, for example, technology has produced the airplane and the rocket; television, the telephone, and the radio have been invented. Yet through all this time, the ma-dake bamboo of Japan, a "century plant," has flowered but once.

The Japanese people greet the <u>phenomenon</u> of the plant's flowering with sadness. The economic life of the country people depends to a great extent upon the ma-bamboo. It is used in making paper, creating art, building houses, and for a myriad of other purposes. Unfortunately, once the plant blooms, it dies. The Japanese people mourn the death of these plants, just as an American farmer would mourn the death of a wheat field.

Since a bamboo forest consists of a single generation of plants, miles of bamboo forests wither at the same time. Plants in a generation go through the various stages of development together.

Most other plants and flowers produce seeds and fruit. But the ma-bamboo is unique in that it sends out roots to perpetuate itself. When the bamboo blossoms, even the roots die, and ten years must pass before new roots take hold.

The last flowering of the bamboo occurred in 1960. In most parts of Japan it will not blossom again until 2060. Like Halley's Comet, it is a rare natural occurrence, to be seen only once in a lifetime—and then only if one is born at the right time.

Main Idea	1	Answer	Score
	Mark the *main idea*	M	15
	Mark the statement that is *too broad*	B	5
	Mark the statement that is *too narrow*	N	5

a. The ma-bamboo blossoms but once in a hundred years. ☐ _____

b. Though the ma-bamboo's blossoms are pretty, they produce sadness. ☐ _____

c. The ma-bamboo is an unusual plant. ☐ _____

Subject Matter   **2**   The subject of this passage is

☐ a. a sad event.

☐ b. the ma-bamboo.

☐ c. changes within a century.

☐ d. unique flowers.   _____

Supporting Details   **3**   Ten years must pass before

☐ a. the flower dies.

☐ b. the flower blooms.

☐ c. new roots take hold.

☐ d. Halley's Comet returns.   _____

Conclusion   **4**   The ma-bamboo is important to the Japanese because it is

☐ a. rare.

☐ b. beautiful.

☐ c. used for many purposes.

☐ d. self-perpetuating.   _____

Clarifying Devices   **5**   In the first paragraph, the writer creates interest in the subject by using

☐ a. precise arguments.

☐ b. amusing narratives.

☐ c. a biased opinion.

☐ d. contrasts of time.   _____

Vocabulary in Context   **6**   The word <u>phenomenon</u> means

☐ a. joy.

☐ b. surprising occurrence.

☐ c. horror.

☐ d. fearful sight.   _____

Add your scores for questions 1–6. Enter the total here and on the graph on page 215.   **Total Score**   _____

6 But It Tastes Good

East coast, west coast, and inland, one of the most popular, and often more costly, items on menus in America's restaurants is the *homarus americanus*. What is this dish that is served so often, steamed or stuffed, in spite of its rather odd appearance? It is the ever-popular lobster.

The lobster looks so strange and <u>hostile</u> that it's surprising anyone first had the nerve to try to eat it. Looking like a large insect, the lobster is actually a cousin of the spider. It has eight spindly legs covered with tiny hairs that detect sounds and smells. When sensing danger, the lobster runs backward.

The lobster also detects food or approaching danger with its two pairs of antennae. When it can't avoid the danger, the lobster wields its two large claws in self-defense. As many lobster handlers have painfully discovered, the lobster can be quite effective in snapping these pinchers.

The lobster's shell is usually a blotchy greenish-black. When it is cooked, it turns bright red. This hard shell, which serves as a barrier to the lobster's enemies, is also a barrier to the lobster-eater's delicious meal. The shell takes time and effort to crack, but the tender lobster meat is worth the work.

In spite of its lack of outward appeal and the difficulty of catching and eating it, the lobster was once almost too popular. For a time, the species was in danger of becoming extinct. But strict laws now require fishermen to release small lobsters and egg-bearing females. So it is less likely that this strange-looking meal will soon be disappearing from our tables.

Main Idea 1

	Answer	Score
Mark the *main idea*	M	15
Mark the statement that is *too broad*	B	5
Mark the statement that is *too narrow*	N	5

a. Popular foods sometimes have visually unappealing characteristics.	B	_____
b. The lobster is a popular food despite obstacles to its enjoyment.	M	_____
c. The lobster can be difficult to eat.	N	_____

Score 15 points for each correct answer.   **Score**

Subject Matter   **2**   This passage is mainly about
- [ ] a. eating in restaurants.
- [ ] b. cooking and eating lobsters.
- [x] c. the lobster's characteristics and popularity.
- [ ] d. how the lobster almost became extinct.

_____

Supporting Details   **3**   According to the passage, the lobster changes color when it is
- [ ] a. shedding.
- [ ] b. in danger.
- [ ] c. removed from water.
- [x] d. cooked.

_____

Conclusion   **4**   The last paragraph suggests that the lobster was threatened with extinction because
- [ ] a. laws made to protect the lobster have not worked.
- [x] b. more lobsters were being caught than were being reproduced.
- [ ] c. the lobster population was decreasing for unknown reasons.
- [ ] d. fishermen were taking only egg-bearing females.

_____

Clarifying Devices   **5**   The writer tells us that the lobster looks like an insect and is related to the spider in order to
- [ ] a. show why the lobster is popular.
- [ ] b. explain why the lobster behaves as it does.
- [x] c. indicate why its popularity as a food may be surprising.
- [ ] d. explain why it has antennae.

_____

Vocabulary in Context   **6**   As used in the passage, <u>hostile</u> is closest in meaning to
- [ ] a. unfriendly.
- [ ] b. timid.
- [ ] c. cautious.
- [x] d. ugly.

_____

Add your scores for questions 1–6. Enter the total here and on the graph on page 215.   **Total Score**   _____

7 A Strange Naval Battle

Arahwe was a strange name for a battleship, but the name was fitting, for the *Arahwe* was a strange battleship. This ship was the only American naval vessel that fought its only battle on dry land. The *Arahwe* was built in the 1860s but never saw action until many years later, when it was traveling along the coast of Chile.

The *Arahwe's* adventure began one day when a massive underwater earthquake occurred right off the coast. Gigantic waves heaved the ship up on dry land, where it was grounded along with several other boats. The *Arahwe* looked helpless and was tempting bait for looters who came on the scene to plunder the shipwrecked boats. When the robbers tried to climb aboard the ship, the crew beat them off with much difficulty. When the looters banded together again for an all-out assault on the ship, the crew knew they were in trouble.

Captain Alexander of the *Arahwe* ordered the gun crew to load the cannon. However, the sailors were unable to reach the cannonballs, which were stored below in the twisted wreckage. Faced with this <u>dilemma</u>, the Captain thought of a substitute for the cannonballs. He ordered the sailors to bring up a basket of hard round cheeses from the kitchen.

When the mob charged at the ship, Captain Alexander ordered the cannons to be fired. Balls of cheese knocked over some of the bandits, and when another cheese round was fired, the mob retreated wildly. After this victory, the *Arahwe* was safe, but it never made it back to sea. It was gallantly listed in the Navy's records as "lost in action."

Main Idea   1

	Answer	Score
Mark the *main idea*	M	15
Mark the statement that is *too broad*	B	5
Mark the statement that is *too narrow*	N	5

a. The *Arahwe* fought an unusual battle. ☐ ____

b. The *Arahwe* fought its only battle on land by firing cheese from cannons. ☐ ____

c. The *Arahwe* was grounded along with some other ships. ☐ ____

Score 15 points for each correct answer.

Subject Matter   **2**   This passage is primarily about
    ☐ a. Chile.
    ☐ b. the *Arahwe*.
    ☐ c. Captain Alexander.
    ☐ d. balls of cheese.   _____

Supporting   **3**   The *Arahwe* was grounded in
Details
    ☐ a. Cuba.
    ☐ b. Florida.
    ☐ c. Chile.
    ☐ d. Brazil.   _____

Conclusion   **4**   Using cheese instead of cannonballs was
    ☐ a. expensive.
    ☐ b. effective.
    ☐ c. sinful.
    ☐ d. wasteful.   _____

Clarifying   **5**   The writer creates interest in the first sentence by
Devices
    ☐ a. telling a joke.
    ☐ b. describing the ship.
    ☐ c. reading from the ship's log.
    ☐ d. talking about the ship's strange name.   _____

Vocabulary   **6**   The word <u>dilemma</u> as used in the passage means
in Context
    ☐ a. problem.
    ☐ b. puzzle.
    ☐ c. mystery.
    ☐ d. crime.   _____

Add your scores for questions 1–6. Enter the total here   **Total**
and on the graph on page 215.   **Score**   _____

8 Count Dracula: Fact or Fiction?

Since 1897 people have been haunted by the story of Count Dracula, the vampire who drank human blood. How much of the Dracula legend is actually based on fact?

Like the Dracula of legend, the real Count Dracula was a fifteenth-century prince who lived in Transylvania, in modern-day Rumania. At first, Count Dracula was called Vlad IV. But his father was known as Vlad Dracul, which meant Vlad the Evil. Eventually Vlad IV himself acquired the name of Dracula, or Devil's Son.

There are several similarities between the real and the legendary characters. The real Count Dracula is said to have been a cruel man who showed no mercy to his enemies. When he captured them, he drove stakes into their bodies—a practice carried over to the fictional Dracula. It was a common belief in Transylvania that the only way to kill a vampire or a devil was to drive a stake into its heart, and that is how the fictional Dracula was finally killed.

Associated with the Dracula tale are vampire bats. Not as dangerous as people believe, bats require only a teaspoon of blood a day to survive. They seldom attack humans; they <u>subsist</u> mainly on the blood of cows and domestic animals. They are more threatening to humans as possible transmitters of diseases such as rabies.

Most legends are based on real events. Stories are passed along from one generation to another until they reach us, usually in a much-changed form. A real event is like an original sound; a legend is an echo. And so it is with the Dracula story.

Main Idea	1		
		Answer	**Score**
	Mark the *main idea*	M	15
	Mark the statement that is *too broad*	B	5
	Mark the statement that is *too narrow*	N	5

a. The real and the fictional Draculas had some common traits. ☐ _____

b. The story of Dracula is based on fact. ☐ _____

c. The real Dracula drove stakes into his victims' bodies. ☐ _____

Score 15 points for each correct answer.

Subject Matter   **2**   This passage is about
- ☐ a. vampire bats.
- ☐ b. the Dracula legend.
- ☐ c. Count Dracula as a cruel man.
- ☐ d. transmitters of disease.

_____

Supporting Details   **3**   A vampire bat
- ☐ a. is very evil.
- ☐ b. can get tangled in one's hair.
- ☐ c. needs only a teaspoon of blood a day.
- ☐ d. attacks humans.

_____

Conclusion   **4**   What conclusion has the author drawn from the facts?
- ☐ a. Dracula was speared with a lance.
- ☐ b. Dracula means "Devil's Son."
- ☐ c. Most legends are based on real events.
- ☐ d. Stories are passed from one generation to another.

_____

Clarifying Devices   **5**   To compare the real and fictional Count Draculas, the author uses
- ☐ a. emotional appeals.
- ☐ b. facts.
- ☐ c. documents.
- ☐ d. arguments.

_____

Vocabulary in Context   **6**   The word <u>subsist</u> means
- ☐ a. to live on.
- ☐ b. to kill.
- ☐ c. to wonder at.
- ☐ d. to ignore.

_____

Add your scores for questions 1–6. Enter the total here and on the graph on page 215.

Total Score

_____

9 The Kingly Monarch Butterfly

Monarch butterflies are a common summer sight in the northern United States and Canada. These large orange and black insects brighten parks and gardens as they flit among the flowers. What makes monarchs particularly interesting is that they migrate—all the way to California or Mexico and back. They are thought to be the only insect that does this.

Every year in the late summer monarchs begin their <u>trek</u> to the south. Those heading for Mexico go first for the Louisiana-Mississippi region, then fly across the Gulf of Mexico into Texas (some have been spotted overnighting on oil platforms in the gulf). Once in Mexico, they establish themselves in one of about fifteen sites in a mountain forest filled with fir trees. Each site provides a winter home for millions of monarchs. The butterflies are so numerous that they often cover entire trees. When spring comes, they begin their long journey north.

The question is often asked whether every butterfly makes the round-trip journey every year. And the answer is no. The average monarch lives about nine months. So one flying north might lay eggs in Louisiana and then die. The eggs of that generation may be found in Kentucky; the eggs of the next generation may end up in Wisconsin or Michigan. The last generation of the season, about the fourth, will make the trek back to Mexico and restart the cycle.

Scientists learn about monarchs' migration by capturing and placing identifying tags on the insects. By recapturing a tagged monarch and noting where it came from, the next scientist can figure out things like the butterfly's age and its routing.

Main Idea	1		
		Answer	**Score**
	Mark the *main idea*	M	15
	Mark the statement that is *too broad*	B	5
	Mark the statement that is *too narrow*	N	5
	a. No other insect except the monarch migrates.	☐	____
	b. Certain insects have very unusual life cycles.	☐	____
	c. Monarch butterflies migrate to California or Mexico every year.	☐	____

Subject Matter   2   This passage is mostly about
- [ ] a. the places where monarchs spend the winter.
- [ ] b. tagging and identifying monarchs.
- [ ] c. migration patterns of the monarch.
- [ ] d. what monarchs look like.   _____

Supporting Details   3   The site in Mexico where monarchs winter is
- [ ] a. a forest.
- [ ] b. a spring.
- [ ] c. a cave.
- [ ] d. a prairie.   _____

Conclusion   4   It seems to be true that most monarchs
- [ ] a. fly hundreds of miles.
- [ ] b. fly thousands of miles.
- [ ] c. need cold weather in order to toughen up for migration.
- [ ] d. fear flying across bodies of water.   _____

Clarifying Devices   5   This passage is mostly developed by
- [ ] a. explaining a natural process.
- [ ] b. telling a story.
- [ ] c. giving a description.
- [ ] d. using examples to prove a point.   _____

Vocabulary in Context   6   A <u>trek</u> is a
- [ ] a. ride.
- [ ] b. path.
- [ ] c. journey.
- [ ] d. detour.   _____

Add your scores for questions 1–6. Enter the total here and on the graph on page 215.   **Total Score**   _____

10 The Last Soldier

Yokoi Shoichi, a Japanese soldier during World War II, never could bring himself to surrender. For 27 years he hid deep in the jungles of Guam, a Pacific island battle site during the war. Shoichi stayed there, away from friends and foes alike, because he felt "shame and dishonor" at the end of the war.

Shoichi knew that Japan had lost the war, but the humiliation of defeat kept him from giving himself up. So he stayed in the jungle, living on what he could scavenge. He consumed mostly insects, snails, frogs, and rats.

In 1972, U.S. authorities finally convinced Shoichi to "surrender." He was sent back to his homeland, Japan. Doctors who examined him there found him to be in good health, with just a touch of anemia due to a lack of iron in his diet.

Shoichi's return home attracted a considerable amount of attention. When a department store in Tokyo exhibited his jungle clothes and tools, more than 350,000 curious people came to view them.

After spending some time back in civilization, Shoichi met a 45-year-old widow. The old solider and the widow fell in love and married. After their wedding, the couple took a honeymoon trip to—of all places—the island of Guam.

Main Idea	1			Answer	Score
		Mark the *main idea*		M	15
		Mark the statement that is *too broad*		B	5
		Mark the statement that is *too narrow*		N	5

a. A soldier who refused to surrender returned to civilization after 27 years. ☐ ____

b. It is often difficult for soldiers to face their country's defeat. ☐ ____

c. Shoichi went into hiding on Guam at the end of World War II. ☐ ____

Score 15 points for each correct answer. Score

Subject Matter 2 The passage is mostly about
- ☐ a. the island of Guam.
- ☐ b. Yokoi Shoichi's marriage.
- ☐ c. the battles on Guam during World War II.
- ☐ d. a Japanese soldier who hid on Guam.

_____

Supporting Details 3 After Shoichi's return 350,000 people in Japan
- ☐ a. met Shoichi when he arrived.
- ☐ b. bought Shoichi's book.
- ☐ c. attended Shoichi's wedding.
- ☐ d. saw a display of Shoichi's clothing and equipment.

_____

Conclusion 4 The passage implies that Shoichi's state of good health upon returning to Japan was surprising because he had
- ☐ a. been exposed to harsh water.
- ☐ b. eaten only the food he could find in the jungle.
- ☐ c. gone for long periods without food.
- ☐ d. had no medical attention for 27 years.

_____

Clarifying Devices 5 The writer mentions Shoichi's honeymoon trip to Guam
- ☐ a. to show how little Shoichi was impressed by modern-day Japan.
- ☐ b. to indicate that Shoichi had not adjusted to civilization.
- ☐ c. because it seems surprising that he would have wanted to return there.
- ☐ d. to illustrate his wife's influence.

_____

Vocabulary in Context 6 In this passage the word <u>scavenge</u> means to
- ☐ a. chew and swallow.
- ☐ b. catch and kill.
- ☐ c. search out.
- ☐ d. break open.

_____

Add your scores for questions 1–6. Enter the total here and on the graph on page 215. Total Score

_____

11 Gruesome Plants

A human-eating plant? Contrary to what you see in the movies, there is no such thing. An insect-eating plant? Yes, there are many such plants, which are as gluttonous in their own way as Hollywood's human-eating variety.

Many carnivorous plants, like the Venus flytrap and the bladderwort, catch their prey with sudden traplike movements. Others, like certain fungi, have nooses or fly-paper-like discs. Perhaps the least dangerous looking yet most deadly carnivorous plant is the pitcher plant, which never has to move to catch its prey.

The American species of pitcher plant consists of a long-stemmed flower surrounded by a slender cone of leaves in the shape of a horn or pitcher. The cone is tipped by a clear protruding <u>canopy</u>. Insects are attracted to the innocent-looking plant by its honeylike scent. After wandering into the cone in search of sweet nectar, the insect soon finds itself sliding slowly down the slippery surface of the chamber's inner walls. Sharp, downward-pointing bristles prevent the struggling prey from moving back up the cone. If the insect tries to fly out, it usually bumps into the transparent canopy and tumbles back into the trap. Waiting for the doomed insect at the bottom of the cone is a pool of fluid that contains a narcotic drug. After it has been immobilized by the drug, the insect drowns and is digested by the bacteria in the fluid. The pitcher then absorbs the vital nutrients.

Main Idea	1	Answer	Score
	Mark the *main idea*	M	15
	Mark the statement that is *too broad*	B	5
	Mark the statement that is *too narrow*	N	5

		Answer	Score
a.	The pitcher plant is a variety of carnivorous plant.	☐	____
b.	There are many types of carnivorous plants.	☐	____
c.	The cone of the pitcher plant is constructed to trap insects.	☐	____

Subject Matter   **2**   Another good title for this passage would be
- ☐ a. Human-Eating Plants.
- ☐ b. The Carnivorous Bladderwort.
- ☐ c. The Death of an Insect.
- ☐ d. The Deadly Lure of the Pitcher Plant. _____

Supporting Details   **3**   What is mentioned as the reason that insects usually can't fly out of the pitcher plant's cone?
- ☐ a. The sides of the cone are slippery.
- ☐ b. Their wings stick to the cone.
- ☐ c. The top of the cone closes over them.
- ☐ d. They hit the overhanging canopy. _____

Conclusion   **4**   The passage implies that
- ☐ a. insects are very observant.
- ☐ b. insects would rather drink nectar than live.
- ☐ c. many insects are eaten by pitcher plants.
- ☐ d. insects learn to avoid pitcher plants. _____

Clarifying Devices   **5**   The phrase "as gluttonous in their own way" implies that carnivorous plants
- ☐ a. eat as much as Hollywood human-eating plants.
- ☐ b. are greedier for food than human-eating plants.
- ☐ c. for their size are as greedy for food as Hollywood human-eating plants.
- ☐ d. are greedy for food, but don't really exist. _____

Vocabulary in Context   **6**   The best definition for the word <u>canopy</u> is
- ☐ a. an overhanging covering.
- ☐ b. a narrow leaf.
- ☐ c. a carnivorous plant.
- ☐ d. the side of a cone. _____

Add your scores for questions 1–6. Enter the total here   **Total**
and on the graph on page 215.   **Score** _____

12 Early Doctoring Practices

Until a century ago, bloodletting was used to treat many <u>ailments</u>. Dating back to before the time of Christ, the treatment involved letting a type of worm, called a leech, suck blood from the patient. People believed that there were liquids called *humors* in the body and that these determined a person's personality and health. Bloodletting, they thought, restored a balance to these humors.

At the time, little was known of the workings of the human body, but people did know that the same liquid, blood, flowed throughout everyone's body. They knew it was a vital substance, for loss of any great amount of it meant certain death. Thus, they concluded that all diseases were carried in the bloodstream, and that if the body was relieved of bad blood, health would return. Bloodletting, however, came to be used as a cure-all. Women were bled to keep them from blushing, while members of the clergy were bled to prevent them from thinking sinful and worldly thoughts.

From the eleventh to the eighteenth centuries, barbers were the people to go to if you needed to be bled. This custom explains the significance of the traditional barber's pole: the white stripes stand for bandages and the red stripes for blood.

Main Idea	1			Answer	Score
		Mark the *main idea*		M	15
		Mark the statement that is *too broad*		B	5
		Mark the statement that is *too narrow*		N	5

a. Bloodletting was once used as the traditional method of curing all illnesses. ☐ _____

b. People thought blood contained liquids called humors. ☐ _____

c. People in the past didn't know much about medicine. ☐ _____

Score 15 points for each correct answer.   **Score**

Subject Matter   **2**   This passage is concerned with
     ☐ a. healthy people and doctors.
     ☐ b. bleeding as a cure-all.
     ☐ c. barbers of long ago.
     ☐ d. leeches with special jobs to do.   _____

Supporting   **3**   The red and white stripes on barber poles symbolize
Details
     ☐ a. sin and redemption.
     ☐ b. the bleeding ritual.
     ☐ c. women who are nurses.
     ☐ d. humors in the body.   _____

Conclusion   **4**   Why is bloodletting no longer considered a cure-all?
     ☐ a. Because more is known about the workings
         of the human body
     ☐ b. Because leeches were outlawed
     ☐ c. Because barbers were too busy cutting hair
     ☐ d. Because today we know that blood is
         necessary for health   _____

Clarifying   **5**   In the second paragraph, the word "thus"
Devices   could be replaced by the word
     ☐ a. When.
     ☐ b. However.
     ☐ c. If.
     ☐ d. So.   _____

Vocabulary   **6**   Ailments means
in Context
     ☐ a. cures.
     ☐ b. women.
     ☐ c. diseases.
     ☐ d. medicines.   _____

Add your scores for questions 1–6. Enter the total here   **Total**
and on the graph on page 215.   **Score**   _____

13 A Fishy Story

Stepping into a puddle of water is common enough, but who could ever imagine stepping into a puddle of fish? In February of 1974, Bill Tapp, an Australian rancher, witnessed a rain of fish that covered his property. How surprised he must have been when he heard the patter of fins hitting against his roof!

What caused this strange occurrence? This is a question that had long puzzled ichthyologists—people who study fish. The answer turned out to be a combination of tornado and thunderstorm.

When it is spring in the Northern Hemisphere, it is fall in Australia. Throughout the autumn season, raging storms arise and rains flood the land. Whirlwinds sweep over Australia like giant vacuum cleaners, collecting seaweed, driftwood, and even schools of fish. Strong gales may carry these bits of nature for many miles before dropping them on barns, livestock, and astonished people.

Although they seem unusual, fish-falls occur quite frequently in Australia's Northern Territory. When Rancher Bill Tapp was asked to describe the deluge of fish, he casually remarked, "They look like perch." His statement is not surprising. The wonders of the natural world are as common as rain. Nature, with its <u>infinite</u> mysteries, can create waterfalls that flow upward and fish that fall out of the sky.

Main Idea	1		Answer	Score
	Mark the *main idea*		M	15
	Mark the statement that is *too broad*		B	5
	Mark the statement that is *too narrow*		N	5

a. Natural weather conditions often cause strange occurrences. ☐ _____

b. A combination of tornadoes and thunderstorms in Australia can produce a rain of fish. ☐ _____

c. Fish-falls occur during the Australian autumn season. ☐ _____

Subject Matter   **2**   What is the subject of this passage?
- ☐ a. The difficulties encountered by ranchers
- ☐ b. A rain of fish
- ☐ c. Australia's Northern Territory
- ☐ d. The damage done by floods   _____

Supporting Details   **3**   Fish-falls occur in Australia
- ☐ a. on large ranches.
- ☐ b. only in the winter.
- ☐ c. quite often.
- ☐ d. when the air is calm.   _____

Conclusion   **4**   What conclusion can you draw from this passage?
- ☐ a. The seasons in the Southern Hemisphere are reversed.
- ☐ b. One should watch where one steps.
- ☐ c. The natural world is full of surprises.
- ☐ d. Ichthyologists are tireless workers.   _____

Clarifying Devices   **5**   Which of the following phrases offers a comparison to describe something in the passage?
- ☐ a. A combination of tornado and thunderstorm
- ☐ b. Whirlwinds are like vacuum cleaners
- ☐ c. Waterfalls that flow upward
- ☐ d. The patter of fins on his roof   _____

Vocabulary in Context   **6**   The word <u>infinite</u> is closest in meaning to
- ☐ a. complex.
- ☐ b. varied.
- ☐ c. countless.
- ☐ d. dangerous.   _____

Add your scores for questions 1–6. Enter the total here and on the graph on page 215.   **Total Score**   _____

27

14 The Terra Cotta Army

You have probably heard of treasures placed in the graves of ancient rulers for use in the afterlife. But no grave site was more impressive than that of Chinese emperor Qin Shihuangdi. This monarch had an entire army buried with him!

Qin Shihuangdi, who ruled in the second century B.C., created the modern country of China. He unified seven independent states that had been warring for centuries. Then he built the Great Wall to keep invaders at bay. The systems of law, government, currency, and measurement that he established remained in place until well into the twentieth century.

When Qin's grave was excavated in 1974, archaeologists found typical royal burial treasures. There was jewelry of gold, jade, and turquoise; there were rare ceramics and coins. But also in the gravesite was a remarkable collection of over 8,000 full-size statues of soldiers, horses, and chariots. This army, made of terra cotta, was lined up in battle formation.

It is not only the size of this clay army that is astonishing. The quality and variety of the sculptures is also impressive. Each soldier's body was made of coils of rough clay and then coated with a finer grade of clay. The head and the hands were created separately. The result was that no two soldiers looked exactly alike. Among the many types of soldiers—all dressed in appropriate, brightly painted uniforms—were foot soldiers, armed chariot drivers, and archers.

Several hundred thousand laborers created Qin's terra cotta army. Their work remained in place, protecting Qin's remains if not his spirit, for over 2,000 years.

Main Idea	1		
		Answer	**Score**
Mark the *main idea*		M	15
Mark the statement that is *too broad*		B	5
Mark the statement that is *too narrow*		N	5

a. Of his many accomplishments, Qin Shihuangdi's terra cotta army is the most impressive. ☐ _____

b. There were over 8,000 full-sized terra cotta soldiers buried with Qin Shihuangdi. ☐ _____

c. Ancient Chinese rulers accomplished remarkable things. ☐ _____

Score 15 points for each correct answer. Score

Subject Matter 2 This passage is primarily concerned with
- [ ] a. Qin Shihuangdi's life and times.
- [ ] b. Qin Shihuangdi's building of the Great Wall.
- [ ] c. the terra cotta army in Qin Shihuangdi's gravesite.
- [ ] d. the work of archaeologists in China. _____

Supporting Details 3 An item **not** found at the gravesite was
- [ ] a. gold.
- [ ] b. turquoise.
- [ ] c. statuary.
- [ ] d. the body of Qin's wife. _____

Conclusion 4 Qin probably had the army constructed
- [ ] a. to war with his enemies.
- [ ] b. to protect him in the afterlife.
- [ ] c. to protect the other treasures in the grave.
- [ ] d. to provide jobs for his people. _____

Clarifying Devices 5 The author of this passage develops the main idea by
- [ ] a. presenting a biographical sketch of Qin Shihuangdi's life.
- [ ] b. discussing various ancient Chinese rulers.
- [ ] c. describing the army found in the gravesite.
- [ ] d. explaining how the army's creators lived and worked. _____

Vocabulary in Context 6 A synonym for terra cotta is
- [ ] a. mud.
- [ ] b. steel.
- [ ] c. clay.
- [ ] d. papier-maché. _____

Add your scores for questions 1–6. Enter the total here and on the graph on page 215. Total Score _____

15 Another Look at Spiders

A good many people hate spiders. Few consider that spiders are intelligent, inventive, and good friends to people.

Spiders have highly developed nervous systems. Their brains are capable of remembering, and they are remarkable engineers. They can be found living anywhere from 22,000 feet above sea level, on Mount Everest, to 2,000 feet below the earth's surface, in caves.

The silk that spiders spin for their webs has a stretching strength superior to most flexible products made by humans. These webs have been known to entangle and hold animals as large as mice. The bola spider, instead of making a web, constructs a silken trapeze, which it hangs from branches or twigs. It attaches a globule of sticky silk to the end of the trapeze and casts it out at passing insects. Any insect that gets stuck to the swinging ball becomes the spider's next meal.

One Eurasian species of spider actually travels underwater by carrying a tiny bubble of air with it. Its home is a cozy diving bell.

Many scientists feel that without the spider human life would be in danger. This is because most of a spider's energies are <u>devoted</u> to catching and eating insects. Without spiders, insects would multiply and cover the earth, destroying the vegetation. One estimate says that each year spiders in England destroy a number of insects equal in weight to the human population of that country!

Main Idea	1	Answer	Score
Mark the *main idea*		M	15
Mark the statement that is *too broad*		B	5
Mark the statement that is *too narrow*		N	5

a. Spiders are highly inventive and extremely helpful to people. ☐ _____

b. Spiders can live and travel underwater. ☐ _____

c. Some creatures are helpful to people. ☐ _____

Score 15 points for each correct answer.   **Score**

Subject Matter   **2**   The best alternate title for this passage would be
    ☐ a. What Spiders Eat.
    ☐ b. The Spider with a Trapeze.
    ☐ c. The Spider—Nature's Great Engineer.
    ☐ d. The Spider's Web.   _____

Supporting   **3**   The bola spider
Details
    ☐ a. lives underwater.
    ☐ b. lives in caves.
    ☐ c. constructs a trapeze.
    ☐ d. catches mice in its web.   _____

Conclusion   **4**   We can conclude from the passage that
    ☐ a. there will soon be more spiders than insects.
    ☐ b. people should appreciate spiders more.
    ☐ c. spiders are smarter than human beings.
    ☐ d. all spiders can live underwater.   _____

Clarifying   **5**   In the sentence "Its home is a cozy diving bell,"
Devices   the writer uses
    ☐ a. a simile.
    ☐ b. an example.
    ☐ c. an argument.
    ☐ d. a metaphor.   _____

Vocabulary   **6**   In this passage <u>devoted</u> means
in Context
    ☐ a. loving.
    ☐ b. given to.
    ☐ c. adoring.
    ☐ d. loyal.   _____

Add your scores for questions 1–6. Enter the total here   **Total**
and on the graph on page 215.   **Score**   _____

31

16 An Ancient Disaster

For more than six hundred years, Pompeii was an important city in the Roman Empire. Located on the Bay of Naples in southern Italy, Pompeii was a favorite spot for wealthy Romans to build their country villas. The city was busy and prosperous, and the streets were lined with shops, houses, and temples. Citizens had use of an open-air theater and public baths. But this dream city had one flaw. Pompeii sat at the foot of Mount Vesuvius.

In A.D. 79, on the morning of August 24, Vesuvius erupted violently. Fire and ash filled the sky and buried the beautiful city. When Vesuvius finally settled down, Pompeii lay buried under pumice nearly ten feet thick. The volcano so changed the area that the spot where Pompeii, a port city, once stood was now two miles from the ocean. Many people died in the great eruption, either from falling rock and collapsing buildings or from the volcano's poisonous fumes. The great city of Pompeii had disappeared.

So it was a great surprise when, in the 1700s, a peasant discovered some statues buried in his vineyard. When people began to dig further, they unearthed the houses, food, and even the bodies of some of the citizens of the once-<u>bustling</u> Pompeii. The city had been covered so quickly that everything in it seemed to be frozen in time.

Main Idea	1		
		Answer	Score
	Mark the *main idea*	M	15
	Mark the statement that is *too broad*	B	5
	Mark the statement that is *too narrow*	N	5

a. The city of Pompeii was once an important city in the Roman Empire. ☐ _____

b. The great city of Pompeii was completely destroyed and buried by a volcanic eruption. ☐ _____

c. Violent volcanic eruptions often destroy cities and kill people. ☐ _____

Score 15 points for each correct answer.   Score

Subject Matter   **2**   Another good title for this selection would be
- [ ] a. Dream City.
- [ ] b. The Great Buried City.
- [ ] c. A Famous Volcano.
- [ ] d. The Story of Vesuvius.   _____

Supporting Details   **3**   The city of Pompeii was a favorite spot for wealthy Romans because it was
- [ ] a. excellent for fishing.
- [ ] b. close to Mount Vesuvius.
- [ ] c. busy.
- [ ] d. located near the water.   _____

Conclusion   **4**   The writer expresses amazement at the
- [ ] a. Roman Empire.
- [ ] b. popularity of Pompeii.
- [ ] c. beautiful city of Pompeii.
- [ ] d. devastating work of the volcano.   _____

Clarifying Devices   **5**   The writer develops the main idea through the use of
- [ ] a. contrast.
- [ ] b. negative arguments.
- [ ] c. vivid description.
- [ ] d. reasoning.   _____

Vocabulary in Context   **6**   Bustling means
- [ ] a. crowded.
- [ ] b. prosperous.
- [ ] c. noisy and busy.
- [ ] d. beautiful.   _____

Add your scores for questions 1–6. Enter the total here and on the graph on page 215.   Total Score   _____

17 The First National Monument

Devils Tower, the first national monument in America, could almost be mistaken for the stump of an enormous tree. Its sheer rock sides sweep up from a broad base until they cut off abruptly at the flat summit. Rising more than 1,000 feet in the middle of the gently rolling plains of Wyoming, the massive column of rock looks as though it was dropped down into this location from a different time and place.

In a sense it was. Devils Tower is a <u>relic</u> of the past, when the molten rock of the earth's core forced its way to the surface to form the throat of a volcano. As the centuries passed the rock cooled and hardened, shrinking and cracking into long columns. Born in fire and fury, Devils Tower was then shaped by the slow, gentle work of wind and water. The outer layers of the volcano were worn away, until the hard core stood completely exposed.

Small wonder that an Indian legend described Devils Tower as being formed by supernatural powers. The legend says that when seven girls were attacked by bears, they took refuge on top of a small rock and appealed to the Rock God for help. The god caused the rock to grow and to lift the girls far above the ground, while its sides were scored by the claws of the angry bears. Even today, says the legend, the girls can be seen above the towering rock, as seven shining stars in the night sky.

Main Idea	1		Answer	Score
	Mark the *main idea*		M	15
	Mark the statement that is *too broad*		B	5
	Mark the statement that is *too narrow*		N	5

a. Devils Tower, the exposed core of an ancient volcano, was the first national monument in America. ☐ _____

b. Devils Tower gradually formed into long columns of rock. ☐ _____

c. One example of a natural rock formation is Devils Tower. ☐ _____

Subject Matter   **2**   This passage is mostly about
- ☐ a. Indian legends.
- ☐ b. petrified trees.
- ☐ c. Devils Tower.
- ☐ d. volcanoes.

       _____

Supporting Details   **3**   What caused the volcano's outer layer to disappear?
- ☐ a. Violent storms
- ☐ b. The cooling of the core
- ☐ c. An earthquake
- ☐ d. Wind and water

       _____

Conclusion   **4**   Devils Tower looks out of place because it
- ☐ a. was built by the Indians as a religious monument.
- ☐ b. is surrounded by open plains, with no other rock formations nearby.
- ☐ c. is much older than other nearby mountains.
- ☐ d. was scored by the claws of angry bears.

       _____

Clarifying Devices   **5**   The author describes Devils Tower as looking like the stump of an enormous tree in order to
- ☐ a. help the reader visualize its appearance.
- ☐ b. explain how an Indian legend was started.
- ☐ c. suggest that it was once a living object.
- ☐ d. emphasize how deceptive appearances can be.   _____

Vocabulary in Context   **6**   As used in this passage, <u>relic</u> refers to a
- ☐ a. holy place.
- ☐ b. leftover part.
- ☐ c. piece of old art.
- ☐ d. reminder.

       _____

Add your scores for questions 1–6. Enter the total here and on the graph on page 215.   **Total Score**   _____

18 An Artistic Mystery

Italian sculptor and painter Michelangelo was one of the most remarkable artists who ever lived. Working in Rome and Florence in the early 1500s, he produced both religious and <u>secular</u> art that is still marvelled at today. But it appears that Michelangelo could be his own harshest critic.

Michelangelo was an old, sick man when he began carving a sculpture known as the Florentine Pietà. (A pietà is a sculpture of the Virgin Mary holding the dead body of Jesus.) He worked on the sculpture only at night, and sometimes was in such pain that he could not work at all. Michelangelo intended to have the huge, almost-eight-feet-high sculpture as part of his own tombstone; included in the work was the figure of an elderly suffering man. In describing the sculpture, Michelangelo's biographer wrote of its great "beauty and sorrow."

But one day, after ten years of labor, the artist suddenly turned on his work. He attacked it with a sledgehammer, chopping off arms and legs. He would have destroyed the sculpture entirely if an assistant had not dragged him away. Later the work was repaired by another assistant, but in an imperfect way.

What prompted Michelangelo to almost destroy one of his greatest works? Did he feel he had made a mistake in the composition or the carving? Did he discover a hidden flaw in the marble? Scientists have begun studying the repaired statue, taking 3-D photos of it from every angle so that they can study its structure on computer. Perhaps someday they will have a clue as to what motivated Michelangelo.

Main Idea	1		
		Answer	**Score**
	Mark the *main idea*	M	15
	Mark the statement that is *too broad*	B	5
	Mark the statement that is *too narrow*	N	5

a. Michelangelo spent ten years working on his huge pietà. ☐ _____

b. Michelangelo unexplainably almost destroyed one of his greatest works. ☐ _____

c. Michelangelo was a remarkable artist. ☐ _____

Score 15 points for each correct answer.   **Score**

Subject Matter   **2**   Another good title for this passage would be
- ☐ a. The Lonely Life of a Genius.
- ☐ b. Michelangelo's Rage.
- ☐ c. Beauty and Sorrow.
- ☐ d. Using a Computer to Reconstruct the Past.   _____

Supporting Details   **3**   Michelangelo was carving the pietà for
- ☐ a. his tombstone.
- ☐ b. a museum.
- ☐ c. a private client.
- ☐ d. an Italian church.   _____

Conclusion   **4**   What conclusion can you draw from this passage?
- ☐ a. Michelangelo was an impatient, temperamental man.
- ☐ b. Michelangelo worked in constant pain.
- ☐ c. Michelangelo ordered his assistant to repair the statue.
- ☐ d. Computers may help in resolving ancient puzzles.   _____

Clarifying Devices   **5**   The author of this passage quotes Michelangelo's biographer in order to show that
- ☐ a. the statue did not look to be flawed.
- ☐ b. Michelangelo was unhappy with his work.
- ☐ c. sometimes biographers don't know what they are talking about.
- ☐ d. Michelangelo could not stand to be criticized.   _____

Vocabulary in Context   **6**   The word secular means
- ☐ a. holy.
- ☐ b. worldly.
- ☐ c. mediocre.
- ☐ d. excellent.   _____

Add your scores for questions 1–6. Enter the total here and on the graph on page 215.   **Total Score**   _____

19 A Well-Balanced Act

Jean Francis Grandet was perhaps the most daring man who ever lived—and perhaps the craziest. His greatest desire was to entertain and amaze people. He measured his success by the number of people who fainted dead away after witnessing his death-defying feats.

Grandet, a blond Frenchman, toured North America in 1850, <u>billing</u> himself as "Blondin." Blondin's gift was superb balance. This talent, coupled with an unquenchable desire to astound his audiences, made Blondin an irresistible performer.

His most famous feat was walking across Niagara Falls on a tightrope. Blondin's "stage" consisted of a three-inch rope strung 1,100 feet across the falls. The rope hung some 160 feet above the jagged rocks and boiling water below the falls.

Simply walking across the falls was not exciting enough for Blondin; he later had to ride across on a bicycle. Then, in another performance, he calmly walked across blindfolded. At still another time, he carried his terrified manager on his back and strolled over the falls before thousands of breathless spectators.

But Blondin was undoubtedly his own worst critic. He was never satisfied with his act and always strove to overthrill his audience with his balancing wizardry. One of his most daring walks was made in the darkness of night. Blondin became so famous on his tour through North America that his last performance was attended by an admiring Prince of Wales.

Main Idea 1

		Answer	Score
	Mark the *main idea*	M	15
	Mark the statement that is *too broad*	B	5
	Mark the statement that is *too narrow*	N	5

a.	Blondin performed death-defying feats that thrilled and amazed audiences.	☐	_____
b.	Tightrope performers amaze audiences by performing fearful balancing acts.	☐	_____
c.	Blondin walked across Niagara Falls blindfolded.	☐	_____

Subject Matter   **2**   This passage is about
- ☐ a. circus performers.
- ☐ b. a balancing daredevil.
- ☐ c. a trapeze artist.
- ☐ d. a foolish Frenchman.   _____

Supporting Details   **3**   Jean Francis Grandet probably performed as "Blondin" because
- ☐ a. he was a show-off.
- ☐ b. he was from France.
- ☐ c. he was blond.
- ☐ d. his manager had suggested the name.   _____

Conclusion   **4**   The passage suggests that Blondin
- ☐ a. was not very intelligent.
- ☐ b. did not like Americans.
- ☐ c. performed as a teenager.
- ☐ d. loved his audiences.   _____

Clarifying Devices   **5**   The writer stimulates the reader's interest by
- ☐ a. using exotic language.
- ☐ b. using a surprise ending.
- ☐ c. describing Blondin's amazing feats.
- ☐ d. asking questions.   _____

Vocabulary in Context   **6**   As used in this passage, <u>billing</u> means to
- ☐ a. charge a price.
- ☐ b. imagine oneself as something.
- ☐ c. spread rumors.
- ☐ d. advertise oneself.   _____

Add your scores for questions 1–6. Enter the total here and on the graph on page 215.   **Total Score**   _____

20 Why Do They Do It?

Why would an animal commit suicide? It seems a strange question, and yet it is one that has intrigued some people for a long time. For there is a kind of rodent, called the lemming, that periodically commits mass suicide, and no one knows just why!

The small creatures, which inhabit the Scandinavian mountains, sustain themselves on a diet of roots and moss and live in nests they burrow underground. When their food supply is sufficiently large, the lemmings live a normal, undisturbed rodent life.

However, when the lemmings' food supply becomes too low to support the population, a singular migration commences. The lemmings leave their burrows en masse, forming huge hordes. Great numbers of the rodents begin a trek across the Scandinavian plains, a journey that may last weeks. The lemmings devour everything in their path, continuing their destructive march until they reach the sea.

The reason for what follows remains an enigma for zoologists and naturalists. Upon reaching the coast, the lemmings do not stop but swim by the thousands into the surf. Most stay afloat only a short time before they tire, sink, and drown.

A common theory for this mass suicide is that the lemmings do not realize that the ocean is such a huge body of water. In their cross-country journey, the animals must traverse many smaller bodies of water, such as rivers and small lakes. They may assume that the sea is just another such swimmable obstacle. But no final answer has been found to the mystery.

Main Idea	1				
			Answer		Score
	Mark the *main idea*		M		15
	Mark the statement that is *too broad*		B		5
	Mark the statement that is *too narrow*		N		5

a. It is unusual for animals to commit suicide. ☐ ____

b. Lemmings periodically march to the sea and drown themselves in vast numbers. ☐ ____

c. Lemmings go on a long march when their food supply gets too low. ☐ ____

Score 15 points for each correct answer.   **Score**

Subject Matter   **2**   The passage is about
☐ a. how lemmings find food.
☐ b. the concept of animal suicide.
☐ c. the phenomenon of the lemming suicide.
☐ d. the food supply in the Scandinavian mountains.   _____

Supporting Details   **3**   A reason for the lemmings' self-destruction might be that they
☐ a. go mad from a lack of food.
☐ b. hope to find fish for food.
☐ c. decide to thin out the population.
☐ d. think they can cross the sea.   _____

Conclusion   **4**   Scientists are intrigued by the lemmings' behavior because
☐ a. they are the only rodents that live in Scandinavia.
☐ b. it is very unusual for animals to commit suicide.
☐ c. of the amount of food they can eat on their march to the sea.
☐ d. they can gather together in such huge numbers.   _____

Clarifying Devices   **5**   The word "however" in the first sentence of the third paragraph signals that the information that follows is
☐ a. merely a detail.
☐ b. in contrast to preceding information.
☐ c. similar to preceding information.
☐ d. an example related to preceding information.   _____

Vocabulary in Context   **6**   In this passage <u>singular</u> means
☐ a. unusual.
☐ b. solitary.
☐ c. temporary.
☐ d. individual.   _____

Add your scores for questions 1–6. Enter the total here and on the graph on page 215.   **Total Score**   _____

21 Thunderstorms

Thunderstorms are one of nature's most common phenomena, events that just about everyone has experienced. Since they are also potentially one of nature's most deadly occurrences, it is a good idea to recognize the conditions that cause them to develop.

For a thunderstorm to form, the atmosphere in an area must have become unstable, usually because of heat developing on the ground or because of a sudden influx of cold air. The first result of this instability is that warm air will ascend and cool air descend. As the warm air goes up, the water vapor within it condenses, and clouds begin to form. More warm air is forced upward and the cloud formation becomes larger and larger, until an enormous cumulonimbus cloud—the kind that generates a thunderstorm—is produced.

Soon the rain begins. When it does, the downdrafting air that it generates mixes with the updrafting warm air. One result of the turbulence this causes is that the air within the storm—and sometimes even the air a few miles away—takes on an electric charge. Conditions are now ripe for lightning to develop. The more charged up the air, the more lightning there will be.

How can you determine how close to you a flash of lightning has struck? The amount of time it takes for a thunderclap to follow is thought to be a good indication. When you see lightning, begin counting slowly. If you can count to five before you hear thunder, the lightning probably struck about five miles away. If you can't even count to three, take cover immediately!

Main Idea	1	Answer	Score
	Mark the *main idea*	M	15
	Mark the statement that is *too broad*	B	5
	Mark the statement that is *too narrow*	N	5

		Answer	Score
a.	Thunderstorms follow a fairly specific pattern as they form.	☐	_____
b.	Any kind of storm is potentially dangerous.	☐	_____
c.	Cumulonimbus clouds generate thunderstorms.	☐	_____

Subject Matter   **2**   This passage is mostly about
- ☐ a. being safe in a storm.
- ☐ b. how thunderstorms develop.
- ☐ c. why lightning is often deadly.
- ☐ d. disastrous thunderstorms in history. _____

Supporting Details   **3**   As a thunderstorm forms, the cold air
- ☐ a. moves along the ground.
- ☐ b. goes up.
- ☐ c. goes down.
- ☐ d. causes lightning. _____

Conclusion   **4**   The shorter the time between a streak of lightning and a thunderclap,
- ☐ a. the farther away is the lightning strike.
- ☐ b. the nearer is the lightning strike.
- ☐ c. the heavier the rainfall will become.
- ☐ d. the lighter the rainfall will become. _____

Clarifying Devices   **5**   The writer develops the main idea of this passage mainly by
- ☐ a. describing kinds of clouds.
- ☐ b. explaining a process.
- ☐ c. telling an exciting story.
- ☐ d. proving a point. _____

Vocabulary in Context   **6**   In this passage, <u>influx</u> means
- ☐ a. a flowing in.
- ☐ b. an elimination.
- ☐ c. a rejection.
- ☐ d. a small amount. _____

Add your scores for questions 1–6. Enter the total here and on the graph on page 216.   **Total Score** _____

22 Rats

Through all of human history, rats have been a curse and a plague to people. They eat or spoil crops of grain and rice before they can be harvested or while they are in storage. In India, where millions of people go hungry, there are ten times as many rats as people. Rats devour half of the available food. Rats will also attack birds and animals, from frogs and chicks to geese and young calves. They have even destroyed dams and buildings by burrowing through or under them. Sometimes they cause fires by chewing on electrical wiring.

The most terrible destruction caused by rats, however, has come from the diseases they carry. In the fourteenth century, rats caused the death of one-third of the world's human population by transmitting bubonic plague. This dreadful outbreak, also called the Black Plague, ravaged Europe for years.

Ironically, it is in fighting diseases that rats have been most useful to humanity. The bodies of rats, though quite different from those of humans, have certain basic structural similarities. So thousands of specially bred rats are used in research laboratories every year to test medicines that can possibly be used to prolong and improve human life. As might be expected, some laboratory rats are even used to test new procedures and methods for <u>eliminating</u> their cousins the wild rats.

Main Idea	1	Answer	Score
	Mark the *main idea*	M	15
	Mark the statement that is *too broad*	B	5
	Mark the statement that is *too narrow*	N	5

a. The Black Plague was a terrible disease carried by rats. ☐ _____

b. Rats cause many problems for mankind, but they can also help with some potential solutions. ☐ _____

c. Animal pests destroy human lives and property. ☐ _____

Subject Matter   **2**   Another good title for this passage would be
      ☐ a. The Black Plague.
      ☐ b. Rats for Good and Evil.
      ☐ c. Common Animal Pests.
      ☐ d. Causes of World Hunger.   _____

Supporting   **3**   The worst disaster caused by rats was the
Details
      ☐ a. starving of millions in India.
      ☐ b. flooding of Holland by the sea.
      ☐ c. spreading of the Black Plague in Europe.
      ☐ d. losing of thousands of homes by fire.   _____

Conclusion   **4**   Which of the following is implied but not stated
in this passage?
      ☐ a. Rats eat their prey alive.
      ☐ b. Rats carry the Black Plague.
      ☐ c. Rats are completely worthless.
      ☐ d. Rats have caused floods.   _____

Clarifying   **5**   The writer mentions the Black Plague as
Devices
      ☐ a. an example.
      ☐ b. a symbol.
      ☐ c. a warning.
      ☐ d. a myth.   _____

Vocabulary   **6**   In this context, <u>eliminating</u> means
in Context
      ☐ a. identifying.
      ☐ b. getting rid of.
      ☐ c. discovering.
      ☐ d. training.   _____

Add your scores for questions 1–6. Enter the total here   **Total**
and on the graph on page 216.   **Score**   _____

23 The Soccer War

Soccer is an extremely popular sport through most of the world. However, as with anything that people feel intensely about, emotions sometimes get out of hand. English fans have been known for brawling in the stands. A riot in a game between Argentina and Chile in 1964 resulted in the deaths of 309 people. But up until now at least, there has only been one out-and-out soccer war.

That war took place between El Salvador and Honduras, two Central American countries. The year was 1969, and for many years the Salvadoran economy had been in a <u>dire</u> condition: too many people with too little land and too few jobs created a situation of severe poverty. As a result, many desperate Salvadorans had been illegally crossing into Honduras looking for work, and they harbored a strong sense that they were mistreated there. So tensions were already very high at the beginning of a World Cup qualifying match between the two countries.

The first game of the three-game play-off was held in Honduras, and the home team eked out a 1-0 win in the last minute of play. Fighting broke out afterward in the streets, and the stadium was set on fire. The second game was played in El Salvador, and the El Salvador team won. More rioting and fires followed. By the time the third game was played, in Mexico City, an actual military encounter appeared inevitable. And that is exactly what happened. Immediately after El Salvador's close victory, armies began skirmishing along the border of the two countries; then El Salvador invaded Honduras and bombed its airfields. The war was over in less than a week, but ill feelings between the two countries persisted for years afterward.

Main Idea	1		Answer	Score
	Mark the *main idea*		M	15
	Mark the statement that is *too broad*		B	5
	Mark the statement that is *too narrow*		N	5

a. Soccer matches between countries often cause hard feelings. ☐ ____

b. El Salvador and Honduras fought a war over a soccer match. ☐ ____

c. Honduras won the first game 1-0. ☐ ____

Subject Matter 2 Another good title for this passage would be
☐ a. Three Deadly Days.
☐ b. Worth a War?
☐ c. Support the Home Team.
☐ d. Winners and Losers.   _____

Supporting Details 3 The number of games the two teams played was
☐ a. one.
☐ b. two.
☐ c. three.
☐ d. four.   _____

Conclusion 4 The author of this passage seems to suggest that
☐ a. soccer fans have no self-control.
☐ b. the Salvadorans and Hondurans were fighting about more than soccer.
☐ c. it is a better idea to have one play-off game than a series.
☐ d. neither team was particularly talented.   _____

Clarifying Devices 5 The writer develops the first paragraph with
☐ a. a summary of the troubles between El Salvador and Honduras.
☐ b. a series of questions and answers.
☐ c. exaggeration.
☐ d. examples of violence related to soccer games.   _____

Vocabulary in Context 6 Dire means
☐ a. dreadful.
☐ b. unnecessary.
☐ c. angry.
☐ d. without rain.   _____

Add your scores for questions 1–6. Enter the total here and on the graph on page 216.   **Total Score**   _____

24 Bird or Mammal?

Classifying animals is not always a simple process. For instance, since its discovery in the eighteenth century, the platypus has been a major problem for biologists and zoologists. This odd-looking creature seems to be part mammal and part bird.

The furry platypus, a native of Australia and Tasmania, looks like a mammal at first glance. But upon studying it more closely, one recognizes the birdlike characteristics that have puzzled scientists. For instance, the platypus has webbed feet like some water birds. It also has a leathery bill like a duck. That's how the animal gets its name, the "duck-billed platypus." In addition, the <u>semi-aquatic</u> platypus lays eggs like a bird.

But once the eggs are hatched, the mother nurses her young, a behavior that is typical of a mammal, not a bird. The platypus has no nipples, however, so the milk is secreted through tiny openings in the mother's stomach, from which the baby laps it up. And even though the platypus has those birdlike webbed feet, at the end of the webs are claws that are similar to those of a cat or raccoon.

After much debate, scientists have finally decided to call the platypus a mammal, just to give it a classification. But it's really in a class by itself.

Main Idea	1	Answer	Score
	Mark the *main idea*	M	15
	Mark the statement that is *too broad*	B	5
	Mark the statement that is *too narrow*	N	5

a.	The platypus has many birdlike characteristics.	☐	_____
b.	Because it has mixed characteristics, the platypus is a difficult animal to classify.	☐	_____
c.	Classifying some animals is neither a simple matter nor a precise science.	☐	_____

Subject Matter   **2**   The passage is mostly about
- [ ] a. animal classification.
- [ ] b. the breeding season of the platypus.
- [ ] c. classifying the platypus.
- [ ] d. the difficulty of classifying animals.

_____

Supporting Details   **3**   The platypus is most like a mammal because
- [ ] a. the female lays eggs.
- [ ] b. it has webbed feet.
- [ ] c. it is semi-aquatic.
- [ ] d. the female nurses its young.

_____

Conclusion   **4**   The difficulty of classifying the platypus suggests that
- [ ] a. classification of animals is not always an exact science.
- [ ] b. only the platypus has characteristics of more than one type of animal.
- [ ] c. most animals have the characteristics of more than one animal type.
- [ ] d. scientists sometimes mistakenly classify animals.

_____

Clarifying Devices   **5**   The writer develops the main idea by depending mostly on
- [ ] a. vivid adjectives and adverbs.
- [ ] b. logical reasoning.
- [ ] c. an emotional appeal.
- [ ] d. a series of examples.

_____

Vocabulary in Context   **6**   The best definition for a <u>semi-aquatic</u> animal is one that lives
- [ ] a. in water or marshes.
- [ ] b. half under water.
- [ ] c. both in water and on land.
- [ ] d. near the edge of a lake.

_____

Add your scores for questions 1–6. Enter the total here and on the graph on page 216.   **Total Score**   _____

25 A Wise Man

He was a funny looking man with a cheerful face, good-natured and a great talker. He was described by his student, the great philosopher Plato, as "the best and most just and wisest man." Yet this same man was condemned to death for his beliefs.

The man was the Greek philosopher Socrates, and he was condemned for not believing in the recognized gods and for corrupting young people. The second charge stemmed from his association with numerous young men who came to Athens from all over the civilized world to study under him.

Socrates' method of teaching was to ask questions and, by pretending not to know the answers, to press his students into thinking for themselves. His teachings had <u>unsurpassed</u> influence on all the great Greek and Roman schools of philosophy. Yet for all his fame and influence, Socrates himself never wrote a word.

Socrates encouraged new ideas and free thinking in the young, and this was frightening to conservative Athenians. They wanted him silenced. Yet many were probably surprised that he accepted death so readily.

Socrates had the right to ask for a lesser penalty, and he probably could have swayed enough of the slender majority that condemned him. But Socrates, as a firm believer in law, reasoned that it was proper to submit to the death sentence. So he calmly accepted his fate and drank a cup of poison hemlock in the presence of his grief-stricken friends and students.

Main Idea   **1**

	Answer	Score
Mark the *main idea*	M	15
Mark the statement that is *too broad*	B	5
Mark the statement that is *too narrow*	N	5

a. Socrates' philosophical beliefs influenced both his life and Greek and Roman thought. ☐ _____

b. Ancient Greek philosophers had a great influence on philosophical thought. ☐ _____

c. Socrates faced his trial and death sentence bravely by sticking to his firm beliefs. ☐ _____

Subject Matter **2** If you were to choose another title for the passage, the best one would be

☐ a. Socrates and Plato.

☐ b. The Trial of Socrates.

☐ c. Socrates' Influence on Philosophy.

☐ d. Socrates: A Man of Strong Beliefs. _____

Supporting Details **3** Socrates was condemned to death because he

☐ a. refused to beg for mercy.

☐ b. was convicted of corrupting the young.

☐ c. founded a school of philosophy.

☐ d. wrote articles attacking the Greek gods. _____

Conclusion **4** By mentioning that Socrates himself never wrote a word, the writer implies that

☐ a. Socrates was not as wise as he is reputed to have been.

☐ b. Socrates claimed the work of his students as his own.

☐ c. it is surprising that his fame and influence were so great.

☐ d. it is possible that Socrates never existed. _____

Clarifying Devices **5** In the first paragraph, the word "yet" indicates

☐ a. the time of an occurrence.

☐ b. confirmation.

☐ c. a contradiction or contrast.

☐ d. that a definition will follow. _____

Vocabulary in Context **6** The word <u>unsurpassed</u> is closest in meaning to

☐ a. not important.

☐ b. not equaled.

☐ c. not noticed.

☐ d. not expected. _____

Add your scores for questions 1–6. Enter the total here and on the graph on page 216. **Total Score** _____

26 King Tut's Tomb

It has long been known that ancient Egyptian rulers, or pharaohs, were buried with great ceremony and lavish treasures that were to be used in the other world. Unfortunately, until 1922 no remains of any of the pharaohs or their treasures had ever been found. In that year, however, an archaeologist named Howard Carter and his sponsor, Lord Carnavon, were at last successful. They found the tomb of King Tutankhamen, who was buried 3,200 years ago. King Tut's tomb was the first fully preserved burial site to be uncovered in Egypt's Valley of the Kings. The two men found the tomb to contain wonderful treasures. Gold figures and magnificent furniture decorated with gold were found in the myriad of secret rooms and tunnels within the pyramid.

The only disappointment for Howard Carter came when he found that King Tut's body was nothing but dust. Apparently a mistake had been made when the king's remains were mummified. Carter did, however, find 143 pieces of jewelry within the mummy case, mostly made of gold and precious stones.

Actually, despite all the publicity about the remarkable finds in his tomb, Tutankhamen's reign as pharaoh was short and relatively uneventful. He died when he was just 18 years old.

There is an interesting story that goes along with King Tut's tomb. According to legend, a powerful curse was placed in it. This curse was to descend on anyone uncovering Tutankhamen's burial place. Not very long after the discovery, Lord Carnavon, along with several of the workmen, died suddenly.

Main Idea   1

	Answer	Score
Mark the *main idea*	M	15
Mark the statement that is *too broad*	B	5
Mark the statement that is *too narrow*	N	5

a. The tombs of Egyptian pharaohs contain great treasures. ☐ ____

b. King Tut's body had not been properly mummified. ☐ ____

c. King Tut's tomb, the first pharaoh's tomb to be uncovered, contained many treasures. ☐ ____

Subject Matter   **2**   The subject of this passage is
- [ ] a. the Valley of the Kings.
- [ ] b. the discovery of King Tut's tomb.
- [ ] c. King Tut's accomplishments.
- [ ] d. Howard Carter, archaeologist.

_____

Supporting Details   **3**   King Tut's body was not recovered because
- [ ] a. his embalmers had made a mistake.
- [ ] b. the Egyptian government would not allow it.
- [ ] c. it had been placed in another tomb.
- [ ] d. the mummified remains were almost 3,200 years old.

_____

Conclusion   **4**   It seems clear that King Tut
- [ ] a. was a great military leader.
- [ ] b. thought a great deal of himself.
- [ ] c. was afraid of dying.
- [ ] d. was killed by his enemies.

_____

Clarifying Devices   **5**   The word "despite" serves to show a
- [ ] a. surprise.
- [ ] b. similarity.
- [ ] c. contrast.
- [ ] d. correction.

_____

Vocabulary in Context   **6**   If you have a <u>myriad</u> of something, you have
- [ ] a. many.
- [ ] b. some.
- [ ] c. few.
- [ ] d. several.

_____

Add your scores for questions 1–6. Enter the total here and on the graph on page 216.   **Total Score** _____

27 Nine Young Prisoners

In 1848, nine young men were convicted of treason against the queen of England. The penalty for this crime was death. These men had to be dealt with strongly, because they could not be allowed to set a bad example for others. Although the people sided with the convicted young men, the judge sentenced them to be hanged.

The court case drew a great deal of public interest, and the nine men became famous. Protests against their punishment were held. Queen Victoria finally decided not to carry out the death sentence, but instead sentenced them to spend the rest of their lives in the penal colonies of Australia.

This change of sentence was fortunate for everyone, because the nine men all went on to become <u>prominent</u> leaders. One had a brilliant career in United States politics, and his son become mayor of New York City. Another, Tom McGee, became a member of the Canadian House of Commons. Two others became brigadier generals in the Union Army during the Civil War. Richard O'Gormon became governor general of Newfoundland. Tom Meagher became governor of Australia, and Michael Ireland succeeded him in that office.

The success of all of the nine men eventually came to the attention of Queen Victoria in a curious way. In 1871 she found herself dealing with the ninth man, the newly elected prime minister of Australia. It was Charles Duffy, a person whom she had saved from hanging. When she heard of the success of the others, she realized that by cheating the hangman she had enriched humanity.

Main Idea 1

	Answer	Score
Mark the *main idea*	M	15
Mark the statement that is *too broad*	B	5
Mark the statement that is *too narrow*	N	5

a. Convicts who are freed can become great leaders. ☐ _____

b. Queen Victoria spared the lives of nine convicted traitors. ☐ _____

c. Nine convicted traitors were spared their lives and became successful leaders. ☐ _____

Subject Matter   **2**   This passage is mostly concerned with
       ☐ a. nine English convicts.
       ☐ b. Queen Victoria.
       ☐ c. the English court system.
       ☐ d. Australia's colonies.   _____

Supporting   **3**   The nine men were convicted of
Details
       ☐ a. robbery.
       ☐ b. murder.
       ☐ c. disrespect.
       ☐ d. treason.   _____

Conclusion   **4**   From this passage we can conclude that Queen
Victoria
       ☐ a. was a cold, unfriendly person.
       ☐ b. never made mistakes.
       ☐ c. never disagreed with anybody.
       ☐ d. was tolerant of human errors.   _____

Clarifying   **5**   To say that Queen Victoria "cheated the
Devices   hangman" means she
       ☐ a. didn't pay the person who would have hung
           the men.
       ☐ b. lied to the hangman.
       ☐ c. robbed the prisoners of their rights.
       ☐ d. cheated death by not hanging the men.   _____

Vocabulary   **6**   Prominent, as used here, means
in Context
       ☐ a. wealthy.
       ☐ b. political.
       ☐ c. energetic.
       ☐ d. important.   _____

Add your scores for questions 1–6. Enter the total here   **Total**
and on the graph on page 216.   **Score**   _____

28 Are You a Good Detective?

Would you like to spend an evening reading a lovely story with beautiful illustrations and make $35,000 at the same time? Millions of people all over the world tried to do just that. Only one succeeded. The book is called *Masquerade,* and it was written by British painter Kit Williams. Within its pages were clues to the location of a golden jewel, and whoever figured out the clues could find and keep the treasure.

This strange tale began when Williams was asked to write a children's book. Wanting to do something no one else had done before, he decided to bury a golden treasure and tell where it was in the book. He began painting without a clear idea of what the story would be about, where he would bury the treasure, or even what the treasure would be. As he painted, he decided that in the story a hare, or rabbit, would travel through earth, air, fire, and water to deliver a gift from the moon to the sun.

After three years, he finished the paintings and then wrote the story. The treasure became an 18-carat gold hare, adorned with <u>precious</u> stones, and it was made by Kit Williams himself. This beautiful jewel, worth about $35,000 (depending on gold prices), was buried somewhere in Britain, free to anyone who could decipher the clues. Williams's assurance that a 10-year-old was as likely to find it as a college graduate helped the book sell millions of copies and kept people of all ages amused trying to solve the mystery of *Masquerade.*

The rabbit was finally found in the spring of 1982 by a 48-year-old design engineer. It was buried in a park about 35 miles from London.

Main Idea	1		Answer	Score
	Mark the *main idea*		M	15
	Mark the statement that is *too broad*		B	5
	Mark the statement that is *too narrow*		N	5

a. The clues in *Masquerade* led the reader to the site of buried treasure. ☐ _____

b. *Masquerade* tells a story of a hare's adventure. ☐ _____

c. Some books lead people on wonderful adventures. ☐ _____

Subject Matter　**2**　Another good title for this passage would be
- ☐ a. British Painters.
- ☐ b. Golden Jewelry.
- ☐ c. A Modern Treasure Hunt.
- ☐ d. Writing Children's Books.　　　_____

Supporting Details　**3**　When Williams began working on his book, he
- ☐ a. was paid $35,000.
- ☐ b. learned to paint.
- ☐ c. had already buried the treasure.
- ☐ d. did not know what the story would be about.　_____

Conclusion　**4**　We can conclude from the passage that
- ☐ a. the clues in *Masquerade* are easy to decipher.
- ☐ b. Kit Williams has many artistic talents.
- ☐ c. many people bury treasures in Britain.
- ☐ d. Kit Williams said he would pay $35,000 to whoever found the treasure.　_____

Clarifying Devices　**5**　The function of the first sentence in this passage is to
- ☐ a. give detail.
- ☐ b. sum up the story.
- ☐ c. capture the reader's interest.
- ☐ d. elaborate upon a point.　　　_____

Vocabulary in Context　**6**　The best meaning for <u>precious</u> in this passage is
- ☐ a. valuable.
- ☐ b. beloved.
- ☐ c. elegant.
- ☐ d. cute.　　　_____

Add your scores for questions 1–6. Enter the total here and on the graph on page 216.　　**Total Score**　_____

57

29 The Amazing Recovery

Some organisms, such as salamanders and lobsters, can regenerate limbs they have lost. This means they can regrow a foot, a tail, or any other part of the body that has been cut or broken off. Although human cells are incapable of this, the human body is wonderfully resilient in other ways. For one thing, it can withstand strong blows and still maintain its ability to function. The amazing recovery of Phineas Gage is a case in point.

Phineas P. Gage, who was employed by the Rutland and Burlington Railroad, recovered from an injury that defied medical history. While he was doing repairs on the railroad, a stock of high-powered dynamite accidentally exploded. The terrific blast drove a three-foot-long, 13-pound iron bar into his head, destroying most of his brain.

Gage was thrown by the explosion, but regained consciousness soon afterward. He even watched the doctors as they tended his wound. For several weeks Gage was disoriented and could not see through his left eye. But after a few months he was able to think clearly and return to work.

Until this day, doctors have found no <u>plausible</u> explanation for this man's recovery. They never expected Gage to survive, but he lived for several years after the accident. After Gage died, his skull was placed in the museum of the Massachusetts Medical College, where it remains as a monument to the human will to live.

Main Idea	1	Answer	Score
	Mark the _main idea_	M	15
	Mark the statement that is _too broad_	B	5
	Mark the statement that is _too narrow_	N	5

a. All living creatures have extremely strong survival mechanisms. ☐ _____

b. Gage withstood a tremendous blow to the head. ☐ _____

c. Gage's story shows that the human body can be tremendously resilient. ☐ _____

Score 15 points for each correct answer.   **Score**

Subject Matter   **2**   This passage is primarily about
☐ a. regeneration.
☐ b. Phineas P. Gage.
☐ c. salamanders.
☐ d. modern medicine. _____

Supporting Details   **3**   Which detail best supports the idea that human beings are very resilient?
☐ a. A few months after the accident, Gage returned to work.
☐ b. Gage's skull is in a museum.
☐ c. Gage was a hard worker.
☐ d. Gage could not see through his left eye. _____

Conclusion   **4**   We can infer from the passage that
☐ a. it takes time to recover from an accident.
☐ b. railroad workers must be careful.
☐ c. the human will to live is powerful.
☐ d. salamanders make good pets. _____

Clarifying Devices   **5**   The author develops the passage by presenting
☐ a. one specific case.
☐ b. arguments and proof.
☐ c. comparison.
☐ d. contrast. _____

Vocabulary in Context   **6**   <u>Plausible</u> means
☐ a. fearful.
☐ b. magical.
☐ c. reasonable.
☐ d. medical. _____

Add your scores for questions 1–6. Enter the total here and on the graph on page 216.   **Total Score** _____

30 A Blaze of Glory

At night you may see a fireball streak across the sky, or a star may appear to burst and fall. These are both examples of meteors—bits of dust or rock from space that burn up and present fiery <u>spectacles</u> as they strike the earth's atmosphere. Occasionally a meteor is so big that part of it survives the journey through our atmosphere and falls to earth. It is then called a meteorite.

In August of 1971, a meteorite crashed through the roof of a storehouse on a farm in Finland. Farmer Tor-Erik Andersson heard a loud noise, and, rushing to the storehouse, found a dark gray rock about the size of a plum. Through its thin crust, Tor could see a concretelike inner core. Tor picked the object up and found it to be unusually heavy for its size. A few months earlier, a similar meteorite had crashed through the roof of Paul Cassarino's home in Wethersfield, Connecticut. This meteorite was a small black rock. It too was unusually heavy for its size. Sky watchers had spotted the meteorite when it was still in the meteor stage. About an hour before it landed in Wethersfield, it was observed as a streak of light shooting through the Connecticut sky. In Monahans, Texas, in 1998, a two-pound glowing white rock whizzed noisily into the front yard of Alvaro Lyles. He and his friends were playing basketball on the driveway at the time.

Meteors are beautiful and exciting sights, and when they come crashing to earth as meteorites they are both frightening and fascinating. Scientists find meteorites very interesting too, because meteorites provide them with an excellent opportunity to study materials from outer space without the expense of space travel.

Main Idea	1			
			Answer	**Score**
	Mark the *main idea*		M	15
	Mark the statement that is *too broad*		B	5
	Mark the statement that is *too narrow*		N	5

a. Meteorites are valuable for scientific study. ☐ _____

b. Meteors and meteorites are bits of dust and rock from space that travel into the earth's atmosphere. ☐ _____

c. Matter from outer space often travels through the earth's atmosphere. ☐ _____

Subject Matter   **2**   In general, this passage is about
- ☐ a. space travel.
- ☐ b. meteors and meteorites.
- ☐ c. watching the sky at night.
- ☐ d. small rocks.

_____

Supporting Details   **3**   One interesting thing about meteorites is
- ☐ a. they always crash through roofs.
- ☐ b. we cannot see them at night.
- ☐ c. they are made of iron.
- ☐ d. they are often heavy for their size.

_____

Conclusion   **4**   From the passage, we can assume that
- ☐ a. meteorites never land in South America.
- ☐ b. not all meteors make it through the earth's atmosphere.
- ☐ c. buildings are flimsy in Finland.
- ☐ d. scientists do not like space travel.

_____

Clarifying Devices   **5**   The writer develops the story by using
- ☐ a. descriptions of real incidents.
- ☐ b. an analogy.
- ☐ c. many statistics.
- ☐ d. negative arguments.

_____

Vocabulary in Context   **6**   In this passage, the word <u>spectacles</u> means
- ☐ a. eyeglasses.
- ☐ b. stage shows.
- ☐ c. displays.
- ☐ d. stars.

_____

Add your scores for questions 1–6. Enter the total here and on the graph on page 216.   **Total Score**   _____

31 The Story of Storks

The story that babies are brought into the home by the stork may have started in northwestern Europe, where the stork is a commonplace sight and is well respected. The stork has white feathers, black wind quills, and a red beak and legs. It stalks fish and other small water creatures in meadows and marshes. Sometimes it is seen in high places such as steeples or chimneys, standing on one leg.

The stork has often been regarded as a sign of good luck. Whenever a pair of storks built a nest on a housetop, the Romans regarded it as a sign of good fortune given by Venus, the goddess of love. The stork was also regarded as a good-luck bird in Germany and the Netherlands. These superstitions persist today. In some places, wheels are put on the tops of houses to give storks nesting places.

Centuries ago, there was already a belief that the stork flew over a house where a birth was about to take place, bringing good luck to the family. The story of storks delivering babies probably arose from this superstition and from many fathers' and mothers' difficulty in explaining to their other children where the new baby came from. It is quite understandable that parents should use the symbol of good luck and the guardian of the home to help explain the arrival of a new member of the family.

Main Idea	1		
		Answer	Score
	Mark the *main idea*	M	15
	Mark the statement that is *too broad*	B	5
	Mark the statement that is *too narrow*	N	5

a. Storks have long been regarded as signs of good luck. ☐ _____

b. There have been many fables about storks. ☐ _____

c. The stork is said to deliver new babies. ☐ _____

Score 15 points for each correct answer.   Score

Subject Matter 2 The subject matter of this passage is
☐ a. ancient fables.
☐ b. good luck signs.
☐ c. nursery rhymes about the stork.
☐ d. legends about the stork.   _____

Supporting 3 The Romans thought storks were
Details
☐ a. rather ungainly birds.
☐ b. signs of good fortune.
☐ c. responsible for babies.
☐ d. only good for eating.   _____

Conclusion 4 The passage suggests that the story of the stork
delivering babies
☐ a. was extremely harmful to children.
☐ b. was an understandable fantasy at the time
it was used.
☐ c. may have been true.
☐ d. was confusing to many people.   _____

Clarifying 5 This passage can best be described as a(n)
Devices
☐ a. myth.
☐ b. informative essay.
☐ c. joke.
☐ d. story.   _____

Vocabulary 6 In this passage symbol means
in Context
☐ a. a loud instrument.
☐ b. something that stands for an idea.
☐ c. a letter or number.
☐ d. an emblem.   _____

Add your scores for questions 1–6. Enter the total here   **Total**
and on the graph on page 216.   **Score**   _____

32 A Natural Contract

It's practically a business arrangement. A symbiosis is a partnership between two living organisms, and it benefits both of the organisms. Nature provides us with many extraordinary examples of symbiosis in the animal kingdom.

It's not an unusual sight in Africa to see a tiny bird, the egret, standing confidently atop the massive back of a rhinoceros. This powerful, and sometimes fierce, animal doesn't at all mind giving the little bird a free ride. Egrets help their larger partners by cleaning them of harmful ticks and fleas. In return, they get a free meal. The relationship between the rhino and the egret constitutes a symbiotic partnership.

Another bird called the plover lives its life happily walking up and down the length of a crocodile's back. The crocodile doesn't object because the plover is valuable to it. The plover frequently crawls into the crocodile's mouth and cleans the huge reptile's teeth. The pickings provide the plover with a meal. The bird's job does not appear to put it in any danger, for the crocodiles never seem to harm the little feathered creatures.

Some symbiotic partners cooperate by sharing a home. For instance, a small blind fish called a goby will often cohabit with a shrimp. The goby keeps the shrimp's tubular burrow clean, and in turn the shrimp <u>procures</u> food for the goby. In all of these examples, each partner benefits from the curious but necessary relationship.

Main Idea   1 ————————————————————————————

	Answer	Score
Mark the *main idea*	M	15
Mark the statement that is *too broad*	B	5
Mark the statement that is *too narrow*	N	5

a. In a symbiotic relationship, two different kinds of organisms help each other. ☐ ____

b. Living creatures help each other in a variety of ways. ☐ ____

c. Egrets and rhinos have a symbiotic relationship. ☐ ____

Subject Matter 2   Another appropriate title for this passage might be
- ☐ a. Unusual Partners in Nature.
- ☐ b. Birds of Africa.
- ☐ c. The Origins of Symbiotic Partnerships.
- ☐ d. Enemies in Nature.

_____

Supporting Details 3   The crocodile provides
- ☐ a. a resting place for the plover.
- ☐ b. transportation for birds.
- ☐ c. a hiding place for the plover.
- ☐ d. food for the plover.

_____

Conclusion 4   It could be concluded from this passage that rhinoceroses
- ☐ a. are frightened by egrets.
- ☐ b. don't harm their egret partners.
- ☐ c. never participate in a symbiosis.
- ☐ d. are gentle animals.

_____

Clarifying Devices 5   The writer explains the meaning of "symbiosis" by giving
- ☐ a. examples only.
- ☐ b. a definition only.
- ☐ c. both a definition and examples.
- ☐ d. several synonyms.

_____

Vocabulary in Context 6   Procures means
- ☐ a. loses.
- ☐ b. carries.
- ☐ c. obtains.
- ☐ d. forgets.

_____

Add your scores for questions 1–6. Enter the total here and on the graph on page 216.   **Total Score** _____

33 The Mad Emperor

Recently a group of historians from all over the world announced its list of the ten greatest tyrants of all time. The unanimous choice for number-one tyrant was Nero, the third-century Roman emperor.

The deranged ruler may have picked up many of his sadistic tendencies from his immediate ancestors. His widowed mother, Agrippina, was the sister of Caligula, the gleeful and insane ruler who tortured and murdered hundreds of Romans. Agrippina married the emperor Claudius. She convinced him to disinherit his natural son, Brittannicus, and make Nero his successor. She then <u>served</u> Claudius poison mushrooms before he could change his mind.

Nero's tyranny was most brutally expressed in his treatment of his own family. Upon ascending the throne at the age of 16, he committed his first recorded murder. He gave his rival, Brittannicus, a fatal potion to drink during a meal. The other guests were alarmed at the youth's death spasms, but Nero called it "an epileptic fit" and calmly went back to eating.

Then Nero dealt with his mother. After she started meddling in governmental matters, he sent her out for a sail in a sabotaged boat. When she survived her ordeal, Nero had her executed.

Nero's marriage also reflected his bloodthirsty personality. His first marriage, to his 13-year-old stepsister, ended when he had her banished and then murdered. He killed his second wife when she scolded him for coming home late. He obtained his third and final wife by having her husband eliminated.

Main Idea	1		Answer	Score
	Mark the *main idea*		**M**	15
	Mark the statement that is *too broad*		**B**	5
	Mark the statement that is *too narrow*		**N**	5

a. Nero was a tyrant and a cold-blooded murderer who ruthlessly killed his own relatives. ☐ _____

b. Nero's family background seems to contain the seeds of his bloodthirsty personality. ☐ _____

c. Throughout history, there have been rulers who were tyrants and murderers. ☐ _____

Score 15 points for each correct answer.   Score

Subject Matter   **2**   This passage is primarily about
☐ a. Nero's family background.
☐ b. Nero's mother, Agrippina.
☐ c. history's greatest tyrants.
☐ d. Nero as a callous murderer.   _____

Supporting Details   **3**   It could be said that Nero followed his mother's example in all of the following except
☐ a. killing a spouse.
☐ b. poisoning a family member.
☐ c. murdering in order to secure a ruling position.
☐ d. killing a brother.   _____

Conclusion   **4**   The passage implies that Nero murdered Brittannicus because
☐ a. they did not have the same political views.
☐ b. Agrippina supported Brittannicus's claim to the throne.
☐ c. Brittannicus was a rival for Nero's wife.
☐ d. Nero feared that Britannicus would attempt to reclaim the throne.   _____

Clarifying Devices   **5**   The writer mentions the historians' naming Nero as a great tyrant in order to
☐ a. point out that this reputation is not deserved.
☐ b. contrast Nero's personality with Agrippina's.
☐ c. give authority to the portrait of Nero as a brutal person.
☐ d. compare Nero with other tyrants.   _____

Vocabulary in Context   **6**   In this passage <u>served</u> means
☐ a. hit the ball, as in tennis.
☐ b. loyally obeyed.
☐ c. gave to eat.
☐ d. waited out.   _____

Add your scores for questions 1–6. Enter the total here and on the graph on page 216.   Total Score   _____

34 Dodgson's Dictionary

Dictionaries are not closed books. There is still plenty of room for more words in these voluminous vocabulary authorities. New words are continually being created and added to our language. And many of today's wordsmiths can credit a famous mathematician with the creation of the method by which they develop many new words. The mathematician was an Englishman named Charles L. Dodgson. In addition to working with figures, Dodgson wrote books. His imaginative stories and poems have made Dodgson beloved to generations of readers. We know him, however, not by the name of Dodgson but by his pseudonym, Lewis Carroll.

Lewis Carroll has delighted countless readers, young and old, with *Alice in Wonderland, Through the Looking Glass,* and numerous poems. In these works, Carroll developed dozens of nonsensical words such as "chortle" and "galumph." Many of these words eventually blended in imperceptibly with more conventional words in the English language. Carroll referred to his made-up words as "portmanteau" words, named after a kind of leather suitcase that opens into two compartments. The name was well suited, because most of Carroll's words had two compartments. Rather than being entirely fabricated, they were usually made from the combined parts of two different words. A "snark," for example, clearly came from a snake and a shark.

Although Carroll died long ago, his technique continues to be used today. We clearly see his influence in such words as *smog, brunch,* and *guesstimate.*

Main Idea 1

	Answer	Score
Mark the *main idea*	M	15
Mark the statement that is *too broad*	B	5
Mark the statement that is *too narrow*	N	/ 5

a. Dodgson, better known as Lewis Carroll, added to our language by forming words from parts of existing words. ☐ _____

b. Charles Dodgson contributed to the English language. ☐ _____

c. Dodgson made up words like "chortle" and "galumph" in the stories and poems he wrote. ☐ _____

Subject Matter 2 This passage is mostly about
☐ a. the book *Alice in Wonderland.*
☐ b. mathematics.
☐ c. how a dictionary is written.
☐ d. how Charles Dodgson created new words. _____

Supporting Details 3 Dodgson's made-up words
☐ a. are borrowed from "real" words.
☐ b. are totally ridiculous.
☐ c. come from Greek.
☐ d. always begin with *s*. _____

Conclusion 4 We can conclude from this passage that Dodgson was
☐ a. better known for his writing than for his work in mathematics.
☐ b. a fine mathematician.
☐ c. perhaps a little crazy.
☐ d. fascinated with dictionaries. _____

Clarifying Devices 5 The first sentence of this passage uses
☐ a. irony.
☐ b. a play on words.
☐ c. a foreign phrase.
☐ d. one of Dodgson's words. _____

Vocabulary in Context 6 A <u>pseudonym</u> is
☐ a. a nickname.
☑ b. a false name.
☐ c. a family name.
☐ d. a foreign name. _____

Add your scores for questions 1–6. Enter the total here and on the graph on page 216.   **Total Score** _____

35 Early African-American Cowboys

Although most TV westerns declined to acknowledge it, many of the early cowboys who helped open up the American West were African American. Brave, talented, and resourceful, they had moved to the West either as freed slaves or as northerners seeking opportunity and adventure. According to one estimate, 25 percent of the cowboys on cattle drives north from Texas between 1866 and 1895 were black. When the era of the great trail drives ended, many continued demonstrating their prowess in rodeos.

Bill Pickett is one of the best-known of the early black cowboys. Born in 1870, Pickett is credited with inventing the stunt of bulldogging, or wrestling a steer to the ground. He first demonstrated the technique in a 1904 rodeo in Cheyenne, Wyoming. It quickly became a staple in all rodeos. Pickett performed for over twenty years in the Miller's 101 Wild West Show. He was inducted into the Cowboy Hall of Fame in 1971.

Other black cowboys are known for other skills. Jessie Stahl, also a Hall of Fame inductee, was a talented bronco rider. After once placing second in an event where he clearly was the best competitor, Stahl mocked the judges by riding a second bronco backward. Nat Love, a former slave from Tennessee, was famous for roping and shooting. Given the name Deadwood Dick after winning several events in a Deadwood, South Dakota, rodeo, Love later wrote an autobiography extolling life in the saddle. These and other lesser-known African-American cowboys were forerunners of black rodeo performers who still thrill audiences today.

Main Idea	1		
		Answer	Score
	Mark the *main idea*	M	15
	Mark the statement that is *too broad*	B	5
	Mark the statement that is *too narrow*	N	5

a. Bill Pickett was a famous African-American cowboy. ☐ _____

b. A number of African-American cowboys were skillful both on the trail and in rodeos. ☐ _____

c. African-Americans made good cowboys. ☐ _____

Subject Matter   **2**   This passage is mainly about
- ☐ a. famous African-American cowboys.
- ☐ b. discrimination in the American West.
- ☐ c. what various rodeo events are like.
- ☐ d. life on a trail drive.

_____

Supporting Details   **3**   Bill Pickett invented
- ☐ a. bronco riding.
- ☐ b. many roping tricks.
- ☐ c. trail drives.
- ☐ d. bulldogging.

_____

Conclusion   **4**   The author suggests that Jessie Stahl did not win the riding contest because
- ☐ a. he was not the best competitor.
- ☐ b. he rode backward.
- ☐ c. he complained about the results.
- ☐ d. he was African American.

_____

Clarifying Devices   **5**   The writer explains the meaning of "bulldogging" by
- ☐ a. comparing it with bronco riding.
- ☐ b. giving a definition.
- ☐ c. stating that it is a compound word and examining its parts.
- ☐ d. giving context clues.

_____

Vocabulary in Context   **6**   The word <u>prowess</u> means
- ☐ a. fame.
- ☐ b. shame.
- ☐ c. skill.
- ☐ d. wealth.

_____

Add your scores for questions 1–6. Enter the total here and on the graph on page 216.

Total Score _____

36 Who's Superstitious?

Many people who achieved great things were superstitious. For example, did you know that Napoleon, the great French general who won countless battles, was afraid of cats? People tend to believe that superstition is linked to ignorance, but this is not entirely true.

Many brilliant people have been superstitious. Rousseau, a famous French philosopher, believed he had a ghost for a companion. William Blake, an English writer and painter, thought he was a brother to Socrates, who had died in 399 B.C.! And Sir Walter Scott would never go to Melrose Abbey when the full moon shone brightly.

Superstitions usually arise when people try to find reasons for things that are beyond their understanding. Primitive societies created all kinds of fantastic explanations for illness, death, and natural events. People looked and wondered at the sky, then developed wonderful stories to account for the various clusters of stars.

Even the age of science has not destroyed people's beliefs in <u>irrational</u> things. The following story is a good example. A panic shook Europe when Halley's comet was expected to appear in 1910. It seemed that whenever this comet had appeared in the past, devastating events had taken place. In A.D. 66, for example, its appearance coincided with the fall of Jerusalem. So the people of the twentieth century feared another catastrophe. They were so frightened that they even bought anti-comet pills and masks to protect themselves from deadly fumes.

Main Idea 1

	Answer	Score
Mark the *main idea*	M	15
Mark the statement that is *too broad*	B	5
Mark the statement that is *too narrow*	N	5

a. Even intelligent and knowledgeable people can be superstitious. ☐ _____

b. Most people are superstitious. ☐ _____

c. Napoleon, who was highly intelligent, was afraid of cats. ☐ _____

Score 15 points for each correct answer.

Subject Matter **2** Another good title for this story would be
- [ ] a. Fear of Black Cats.
- [ ] b. Napoleon the General.
- [ ] c. Superstition and Intelligence.
- [ ] d. Panic in Europe. _____

Supporting Details **3** William Blake was
- [ ] a. Napoleon's friend.
- [ ] b. a French philosopher.
- [ ] c. an English writer.
- [ ] d. a brother to Socrates. _____

Conclusion **4** This passage suggests that
- [ ] a. superstitious people are not always ignorant.
- [ ] b. anti-comet pills are effective.
- [ ] c. people panic too easily.
- [ ] d. Socrates was a brilliant Greek philosopher. _____

Clarifying Devices **5** The writer develops the main idea primarily through the use of
- [ ] a. descriptions.
- [ ] b. historical examples.
- [ ] c. comparisons.
- [ ] d. anecdotes. _____

Vocabulary in Context **6** As used in this passage, the word <u>irrational</u> means
- [ ] a. not reasonable.
- [ ] b. silly.
- [ ] c. unimportant.
- [ ] d. general. _____

Add your scores for questions 1–6. Enter the total here and on the graph on page 216. **Total Score** _____

37 The *Titanic's* Sisters

These days everyone knows about the *Titanic,* the gigantic luxury liner that sunk in 1912 on its maiden voyage. Fewer people, however, have heard of the *Titanic's* two sister ships, the *Olympic* and the *Britannic,* and what fate befell them.

The *Olympic* was the first of the three liners to be built. Originally launched in 1910, it was the largest ship in the world at that time and almost as luxurious as the *Titanic* would be. After the *Titanic* disaster the ship was retrofitted with additional lifeboats and a stronger bottom and then sent back into passenger service. Not long after World War I began, the *Olympic* was again transformed—this time into a naval transport ship. The *Olympic* was attacked by German U-boats four separate times but always managed to escape. One time she even turned and rammed an attacking submarine, sinking it in the process.

After the war the *Olympic* returned to passenger service. By the time she was scrapped in 1935, she had transported over 40,000 passengers and about 66,000 troops.

In contrast to the reliable *Olympic,* the *Britannic's* history is more like the *Titanic's.* Completed in 1914, the ship had many safety features that the *Titanic* lacked. But on its fourth voyage as a troop transporter—the only type of passenger it ever carried—the *Britannic* sank less than an hour after an explosion, caused by a mine or torpedo, ripped open its bow. Thanks to its many lifeboats, nearly all aboard escaped. But carelessly left open were the doors dividing its hull into water-tight compartments. Might the *Britannic* have survived had they been closed?

Main Idea	1		
		Answer	Score
	Mark the *main idea*	M	15
	Mark the statement that is *too broad*	B	5
	Mark the statement that is *too narrow*	N	5

a. Many luxury ships were put to wartime service. ☐ _____

b. The *Olympic* was retrofitted after the *Titanic* sank. ☐ _____

c. The *Olympic* and the *Britannic* were both similar to and different from the *Titanic.* ☐ _____

Subject Matter   2   Another good title for this story would be
- [ ] a. Three Tragic Ships.
- [ ] b. The Results of War.
- [ ] c. Three Sisters, Different Lives.
- [ ] d. The Unsinkable Three.

_____

Supporting Details   3   Both the *Olympic* and the *Britannic*
- [ ] a. sank in wartime.
- [ ] b. carried troops.
- [ ] c. carried wealthy passengers.
- [ ] d. were built after the *Titanic*.

_____

Conclusion   4   The *Britannic* was originally designed to be
- [ ] a. a twin of the *Titanic*.
- [ ] b. a troop transporter.
- [ ] c. a luxury ship.
- [ ] d. the largest ship in the world.

_____

Clarifying Devices   5   The last sentence in this passage is intended to
- [ ] a. make the reader think.
- [ ] b. raise a question that the writer will answer in another passage.
- [ ] c. prove that the ship's crew was negligent.
- [ ] d. summarize the content of the passage.

_____

Vocabulary in Context   6   As used in this passage, the word <u>scrapped</u> means
- [ ] a. removed the finish from.
- [ ] b. fought with.
- [ ] c. put out of use.
- [ ] d. given new parts.

_____

Add your scores for questions 1–6. Enter the total here and on the graph on page 216.   **Total Score**   _____

38 Victorious Crickets

Crickets, in the ordinary scheme of things, are unexceptional insects. But in ancient China crickets were the stars of a national pastime. They functioned as highly trained athletes.

People would search the fields vigorously for the biggest and strongest crickets that could be found. Then these carefully selected crickets were cared for according to a regular routine. They were always well fed, to keep them strong and heavy, and they were prodded into exercising by being forced to jump and jump until they were exhausted. In this manner, the crickets' muscles were built up to far beyond ordinary cricket strength. When the owner-trainers felt their crickets were in tip-top shape, they would announce a challenge. A public bout would take place.

Like the gladiators of Rome, crickets were forced to face each other in high-stake duels to the death. They were placed in a small pit, and a referee irritated their sensitive antennae to goad them into attacking one another. The insects would scuttle toward one another and attempt to rip each other apart. The survivor, of course, was a much celebrated and applauded insect, especially if several bets had been placed on it and the cricket had earned some members of the audience a few dollars. Extremely successful crickets could be sold for roughly $100 each, and there was a rumor that one cricket made over $90,000 in winnings for its owner. When this champion of champions died, it was <u>interred</u> in a miniature silver coffin and given the honorable title "Victorious Cricket."

Main Idea 1

	Answer	Score
Mark the *main idea*	M	15
Mark the statement that is *too broad*	B	5
Mark the statement that is *too narrow*	N	5

a. In ancient China, cricket dueling was a form of amusement and a basis for betting. ☐ _____

b. Successful crickets were sold for high prices. ☐ _____

c. In ancient China, crickets provided a popular form of entertainment. ☐ _____

Subject Matter   **2**   The topic of this passage is
- [ ] a. famous pet crickets.
- [ ] b. dueling crickets.
- [ ] c. Chinese customs.
- [ ] d. a dead champion.   _____

Supporting Details   **3**   "Victorious Cricket" was buried in a
- [ ] a. pet cemetery.
- [ ] b. country cemetery.
- [ ] c. tiny silver coffin.
- [ ] d. small grave.   _____

Conclusion   **4**   In the third paragraph, the author implies that crickets were
- [ ] a. armed with sharp spurs.
- [ ] b. not willing to fight of their own accord.
- [ ] c. not very vicious fighters.
- [ ] d. rewarded with a good meal.   _____

Clarifying Devices   **5**   The phrase "of course" in the third paragraph identifies an
- [ ] a. easily answered question.
- [ ] b. argument.
- [ ] c. obvious statement.
- [ ] d. expected comparison.   _____

Vocabulary in Context   **6**   The word <u>interred</u> means
- [ ] a. pasted on.
- [ ] b. buried.
- [ ] c. set adrift on a stream.
- [ ] d. encased in concrete.   _____

Add your scores for questions 1–6. Enter the total here and on the graph on page 216.   **Total Score**   _____

39 Life in the Deep

Strange-looking creatures dwell in the deepest parts of the ocean, where no light ever reaches. One of the inhabitants of this dark, high-pressure underwater <u>habitat</u> is the anglerfish. It has several unusual features.

Since it is so dark in the depths of Davy Jones's Locker, it is very difficult for fish to spot possible prey or to find mates. The female anglerfish solves the hunting problem by means of a long tentacle up to four inches in length that extends upward from the top of her body. This tentacle acts as a fishing pole of sorts: its end emits a glowing light that in the pitch darkness serves to attract smaller fish. At the appropriate moment, the female anglerfish quickly snaps up her prey.

Nature has apparently solved the anglerfish's problem of finding a mate by developing a relationship in which the male of the species acts as a parasite to the female. The much smaller male anglerfish attaches itself to a female early in its life by biting into her flesh. His mouth becomes firmly affixed to the female's skin, and soon they are even sharing the same bloodstream! After this stage has been reached, the male receives its nourishment through the connection to the female, and soon its own digestive organs and other major organs deteriorate. Only the reproductive organs remain intact.

Main Idea   1

	Answer	Score
Mark the *main idea*	M	15
Mark the statement that is *too broad*	B	5
Mark the statement that is *too narrow*	N	5

a. The anglerfish has special adaptations that help it live in the darkness of the ocean's depths. ☐ ____

b. Strange-looking creatures live in the depths of the sea. ☐ ____

c. The female anglerfish has a special way of attracting other fish. ☐ ____

Score 15 points for each correct answer.

Subject Matter   2   This passage deals mainly with
- ☐ a. deep-sea life.
- ☐ b. interesting facts about anglerfish.
- ☐ c. nature's way of solving problems of environment.
- ☐ d. the diet of the anglerfish.   _____

Supporting Details   3   The anglerfish uses its tentacle to
- ☐ a. attract food.
- ☐ b. communicate with other anglerfish.
- ☐ c. light up the ocean so it can find its way.
- ☐ d. blend in with the seaweed.   _____

Conclusion   4   It can be assumed from the passage that
- ☐ a. the male anglerfish dies before the female.
- ☐ b. the mate-finding problem is solved because the mates remain attached to each other.
- ☐ c. the small prey of the anglerfish cannot escape once they are drawn to the light.
- ☐ d. anglerfish are the biggest in the deep sea.   _____

Clarifying Devices   5   The anglerfish's "hunting problem," referred to in the second paragraph, is the problem of
- ☐ a. finding a mate.
- ☐ b. finding fish to eat.
- ☐ c. being hunted by larger fish.
- ☐ d. being caught by fisherman.   _____

Vocabulary in Context   6   The word <u>habitat</u> means
- ☐ a. living environment.
- ☐ b. dangerous area.
- ☐ c. dark area.
- ☐ d. ocean bed.   _____

Add your scores for questions 1–6. Enter the total here and on the graph on page 216.   **Total Score**   _____

40 Forced to Try Anything

The instinct for self-preservation is a strong one and can inspire some unusual behavior. During the 14th century, the infamous plague called the Black Death raged through Europe. Fear of contamination motivated people to try many strange things in order to save themselves.

In Lubeck, Germany, the panicked citizens believed the plague was a <u>manifestation</u> of the wrath of God. They tried to appease this anger by bringing money and riches to the churches. At one church, the monks, fearing contamination themselves, would not let the people enter. So the crowd threw their gold and jewels over the walls only to have them tossed back by the cautious priests. The valuables were finally allowed to pile up, but they remained untouched for months.

During this epidemic, people tried every imaginable preventative remedy. Many people believed that sitting between two great fires might be a preventative. There was an attempt to wipe out the swallow population, because it was widely believed that swallows transmitted the disease. Allowing birds to fly about the sickroom was also tried, on the theory that the birds would absorb the airborne poisons.

All varieties of unpleasant substances were used in the belief that they would help to prevent or cure the plague. These attempts ranged from smoking tobacco to placing dried toads or the insides of pigeons or newborn puppies over the boils caused by the disease. Interestingly, smoking may actually have had some positive effect. Smoke drove away the plague-bearing flies.

Main Idea	1		Answer	Score
	Mark the *main idea*		M	15
	Mark the statement that is *too broad*		B	5
	Mark the statement that is *too narrow*		N	5
	a. The instinct for survival is very strong.		☐	_____
	b. The desire to avoid the plague caused some unusual behavior.		☐	_____
	c. Smoking may have helped to save some people from the plague.		☐	_____

Subject Matter   **2**   The best alternate title for this passage would be
- ☐ a. Smoking and the Plague.
- ☐ b. Causes of the Black Plague.
- ☐ c. An Incident at Lubeck.
- ☐ d. The Fear of Contamination. _____

Supporting Details   **3**   During the plague, some people brought birds into the sickroom because they believed they
- ☐ a. were a sign of good luck.
- ☐ b. carried the plague.
- ☐ c. carried antibodies for the disease.
- ☐ d. absorbed poisons in the air. _____

Conclusion   **4**   The second paragraph implies that
- ☐ a. the instinct for survival is stronger than greed.
- ☐ b. rich and powerful persons have special immunity to disease.
- ☐ c. people are overly cautious about contagious diseases.
- ☐ d. the wrath of God brought on the plague. _____

Clarifying Devices   **5**   The main idea of this passage is developed mainly though the use of
- ☐ a. deductive reasoning.
- ☐ b. examples.
- ☐ c. comparison.
- ☐ d. logical arguments. _____

Vocabulary in Context   **6**   A <u>manifestation</u> is
- ☐ a. a procession.
- ☐ b. a question.
- ☐ c. a display.
- ☐ d. an example. _____

Add your scores for questions 1–6. Enter the total here and on the graph on page 216.   **Total Score** _____

41 The World's Bloodiest Acre

The Roman Colosseum has been hailed as a "vision of beauty." Michelangelo is said to have wandered there "to lift his soul," and many tourists still flock to see the majestic ruins. Built over 1,900 years ago, this amphitheater is often looked upon as a symbol of human artistry and intellect. But the history of what took place there reveals a dark side of human nature: this site of splendor was once home to a carnival of carnage.

The Emperor Vespasian, who began the Colosseum's construction, did not live to see its completion, but his son, Titus, did. It was Titus who began the bloody "games" that were held in the great ring of the Colosseum for over 400 years. Ceremonies held by Titus to inaugurate the structure lasted for 100 days. In these, beast was <u>pitted</u> against beast, man against beast, and man against man, in battles to the death.

For the next 300 years, a number of programs similar to, but more modest than, Titus's continued to be held at the Colosseum. Bloodthirsty spectators often clamored for "the game without end," a never-ending bout in which an armed man slaughtered a defenseless opponent. The victor of each contest was then disarmed and became the victim of another armed participant.

In A.D. 404 human contests were finally banned, but for another hundred years animals continued to be slaughtered in the Colosseum for the entertainment of the Roman populace. The arena's gory history has prompted one writer to call it "The World's Bloodiest Acre."

Main Idea	1		
		Answer	**Score**
Mark the *main idea*		M	15
Mark the statement that is *too broad*		B	5
Mark the statement that is *too narrow*		N	5

a. The Colosseum was the site of centuries of bloody forms of entertainment. ☐ _____

b. Society in ancient Rome enjoyed bloody pastimes. ☐ _____

c. After its completion, there was a gory 100-day celebration at the Colosseum. ☐ _____

Subject Matter   2   The passage is primarily about
- ☐ a. Emperor Titus's first 100 days as emperor.
- ☐ b. the construction of the Colosseum.
- ☐ c. the competitions held in the Colosseum.
- ☐ d. the beauty of the Colosseum.   _____

Supporting Details   3   According to the passage, what entertainment was particularly popular with the Roman spectators?
- ☐ a. the slaughtering of animals
- ☐ b. beast in competition against beast
- ☐ c. man in competition against beast
- ☐ d. the game without end   _____

Conclusion   4   The first paragraph of the passage implies that
- ☐ a. the Colosseum is not as beautiful as most people believe.
- ☐ b. tourists have destroyed the Colosseum.
- ☐ c. the passage of time has ruined the beauty of the Colosseum.
- ☐ d. the history of the Colosseum was not beautiful.   _____

Clarifying Devices   5   The phrase "a dark side of human nature" refers to
- ☐ a. ancient human accomplishments.
- ☐ b. human history during the Dark Ages.
- ☐ c. human cruelty.
- ☐ d. ancient human competition.   _____

Vocabulary in Context   6   In this passage <u>pitted</u> means
- ☐ a. full of dents.
- ☐ b. set against.
- ☐ c. put in holes.
- ☐ d. thrown.   _____

Add your scores for questions 1–6. Enter the total here and on the graph on page 217.   **Total Score**   _____

42 How Hollywood Went "Hollywood"

The land of tinsel and glitter hasn't always shone as brightly as it does today. For most people, Hollywood is synonymous with movies, glamour, and fast living. Yet this commonly held image could not be more diametrically opposed to what the town's founders intended.

Horace Wilcox, the leader of the Temperance Society, was one of the early developers of the area; in fact, his wife gave Hollywood its name. After acquiring the land for the community in 1887, Wilcox established an orchard, built homes and churches, and planned for parks and libraries. Intending the village to be a model community, Wilcox and the Society declared that only those who <u>abstained</u> from alcohol could settle there.

Hollywood existed as its founders intended for over 20 years. In 1900 there were fewer than 500 residents. No one carried firearms and there was no jail, as crime was practically nonexistent. The mayor served without pay as a public service, and the town's trustees held only a single annual meeting.

But this quiet and bliss were destined to end. In 1910 the residents voted to join with the city of Los Angeles in order to gain access to the city's water supply. The following year, the first motion picture studio was established, and from then on the industry grew rapidly.

Hollywood today is universally considered the movie capital of the world. With its large population and its image of opulence and excess, the city is a far cry from the small temperance community of its origins.

Main Idea	1	Answer	Score
	Mark the *main idea*	M	15
	Mark the statement that is *too broad*	B	5
	Mark the statement that is *too narrow*	N	5

		Answer	Score
a.	In the early 1900s, Hollywood was a small town.	☐	____
b.	Hollywood has become a very different community from what its founders intended.	☐	____
c.	Like many towns that were once small, Hollywood has changed.	☐	____

Score 15 points for each correct answer. Score

Subject Matter 2 The best alternate title for the passage would be
☐ a. Horace Wilcox, Founder of Hollywood.
☐ b. Hollywood—Then and Now.
☐ c. The Temperance Movement.
☐ d. Hollywood—Movie Capital of the World. _____

Supporting Details 3 Hollywood was named by
☐ a. Horace Wilcox.
☐ b. members of the Temperance Society.
☐ c. the early residents of the town.
☐ d. Horace Wilcox's wife. _____

Conclusion 4 According to the passage, what event seems to have opened the way for movie studios in Hollywood?
☐ a. the expansion of the movie industry
☐ b. Horace Wilcox's death
☐ c. the residents' vote to join the city of Los Angeles
☐ d. a sudden growth in Hollywood's population _____

Clarifying Devices 5 As used in the first paragraph, "yet" indicates
☐ a. an explanation.
☐ b. a contrasting idea.
☐ c. a similar event.
☐ d. an example. _____

Vocabulary in Context 6 Abstained means
☐ a. didn't sell.
☐ b. didn't like the taste of.
☐ c. refrained from using.
☐ d. used wisely. _____

Add your scores for questions 1–6. Enter the total here and on the graph on page 217. Total Score _____

43 Eyeglasses

How long ago were eyeglasses first used? Theodore Roosevelt was the first president to pose for his official portrait in glasses. Benjamin Franklin wore wire-rimmed eyeglasses in the 1700s; he also invented bifocals. As long ago as the 1600s, the famous philosopher Spinoza made lenses for glasses. It was at the beginning of that century that the astronomer Galileo used ground glass, in the form of a telescope, to aid the human eye in exploring the hidden details of the universe.

Eyeglasses, in fact, were invented as long ago as the 1300s. Eyeglasses may seem out of place on a figure painted in the Middle Ages, but at that time glasses were considered the mark of a person of learning, of someone worthy of respect. In 1480 the Italian painter Domenico Ghirlandajo painted a portrait of St. Jerome in which he included spectacles hanging from the saint's desk. Such a detail is remarkable, since St. Jerome had died over a thousand years earlier! Although St. Jerome could not possibly have worn glasses, the artist appended them as a symbol of special dignity. The spectacle-maker's guild even made St. Jerome its patron saint.

Spectacles today are made of both glass and plastic. They may be tinted, sunsensitive, reflective, or cut into fanciful shapes. Contact lenses may be worn invisibly, directly on the eyes, and are often now sold in disposable varieties. All of these vision improvers are a far cry from the crude, heavy eyeglasses of the 14th century!

Main Idea	1		
		Answer	Score
	Mark the *main idea*	M	15
	Mark the statement that is *too broad*	B	5
	Mark the statement that is *too narrow*	N	5

a. Eyeglasses have a long history, extending back to the 1300s. ☐ _____

b. Eyeglasses were invented long ago. ☐ _____

c. Eyeglasses have become very sophisticated. ☐ _____

Subject Matter   2   Another good title for this passage would be
- [ ] a. Ben Franklin's Invention.
- [ ] b. The History of Eyeglasses.
- [ ] c. How Far Can People See?
- [ ] d. Galileo's Glasses.

_____

Supporting Details   3   This passage mentions that Benjamin Franklin invented
- [ ] a. bifocals.
- [ ] b. the telescope.
- [ ] c. the first eyeglasses.
- [ ] d. the lightning rod.

_____

Conclusion   4   According to information in this passage, St. Jerome died somewhere around
- [ ] a. 1300.
- [ ] b. 1480.
- [ ] c. 480.
- [ ] d. 1600.

_____

Clarifying Devices   5   In the first paragraph, historical figures are listed in
- [ ] a. order of importance.
- [ ] b. random sequence.
- [ ] c. alphabetical order.
- [ ] d. reverse historical order.

_____

Vocabulary in Context   6   Appended as used in this passage means
- [ ] a. upset.
- [ ] b. added.
- [ ] c. cut out.
- [ ] d. painted.

_____

Add your scores for questions 1–6. Enter the total here and on the graph on page 217.   **Total Score**   _____

44 The Charge of O'Higgins's Brigade

The South American nation of Chile can credit its independence to the military expertise of a herd of sheep, cow, mules, and dogs—and to the brilliant plan of Bernardo O'Higgins, the country's first ruler.

In 1814, Bernardo O'Higgins was the renegade leader of a small group of Chileans who were rebelling against their Spanish rulers. The Spanish outnumbered the courageous patriots and slowly but surely drove the Chileans into retreat. By October 1814 the Spanish had successfully surrounded O'Higgins and his weary followers. When O'Higgins was wounded in battle, morale dropped drastically, and it seemed that only a miracle could have saved the surrounded <u>band</u>. So O'Higgins arranged for one.

O'Higgins had his soldiers round up all the farm animals in the area, then arranged his troops directly behind the confused ranks of the animal army. When he suddenly gave the order to charge, the noise, the shouting, and the firing of weapons panicked the animals, and they stampeded wildly toward the Spanish lines.

The battle-hardened Spanish army was not easily frightened, but the sight of hundreds of stampeding beasts was too much for them. The Spanish lines broke in wild confusion.

O'Higgins and his men charged through the gap in the enemy lines and were safely in the hills before the Spanish recovered from the shock. Their escape provided the patriots with the chance to regroup. Bernardo O'Higgins returned to battle and defeated the Spanish in 1818.

Main Idea	1		
		Answer	Score
Mark the *main idea*		M	15
Mark the statement that is *too broad*		B	5
Mark the statement that is *too narrow*		N	5

a. Bernardo O'Higgins was the leader of a small group of Chilean patriots. ☐ _____

b. Creative thinking can help people win battles against strong odds. ☐ _____

c. Bernardo O'Higgins helped Chile gain its independence by tricking the enemy Spanish. ☐ _____

Subject Matter   2   The subject of this passage is
- [ ] a. the Spanish-American War.
- [ ] b. Spanish conquests in South America.
- [ ] c. how farm animals helped Chile gain its independence.
- [ ] d. the plight of the Spanish army.

_____

Supporting Details   3   The Chilean patriots were at a disadvantage because they were
- [ ] a. poor soldiers.
- [ ] b. outnumbered.
- [ ] c. on unfamiliar ground.
- [ ] d. short of horses.

_____

Conclusion   4   One could conclude from this passage that Bernardo O'Higgins was
- [ ] a. a paid fighter.
- [ ] b. a trained general.
- [ ] c. a native Chilean.
- [ ] d. an imaginative man.

_____

Clarifying Devices   5   The writer
- [ ] a. tells a fable.
- [ ] b. gives a historical account.
- [ ] c. gives an eyewitness account.
- [ ] d. thinks O'Higgins was lucky.

_____

Vocabulary in Context   6   In this passage band means
- [ ] a. a musical group.
- [ ] b. a group of people.
- [ ] c. a thin ring.
- [ ] d. a song on a record.

_____

Add your scores for questions 1–6. Enter the total here and on the graph on page 217.   **Total Score**   _____

45 Stronger Than an Elephant

The jungles of Southeast Asia are home to one of the largest snakes in the world: the regal, or reticulated, python. These snakes can grow to be more than 30 feet long and rank among the strongest animals in existence. A python does not, however, actually crush its prey; it catches its victims by waiting in ambush, its long spotted body masquerading as a vine or tree trunk. When a monkey or pig comes close, the python attacks by wrapping several coils of its body around the <u>hapless</u> animal. Then the snake slowly tightens the coils every time the animal breathes out, until it has suffocated its prey.

The most astonishing part of the python's hunting method is the way in which it eats its prey, for it has no arms or legs, and its teeth, although sharp, are quite thin and delicate. The trick is that the snake can stretch its neck to many times its usual diameter, it can move the two halves of its lower jaw separately from each other, and its teeth curve backward. Starting at the prey's head, the python actually pulls itself over the victim by sliding one jaw forward and sinking in the teeth on that side, and using that position as an anchor to pull the other jaw forward until the entire body of its catch has been swallowed. Methodically following this procedure, pythons have been known to ingest animals as large as pigs!

Main Idea	1		
		Answer	**Score**
	Mark the _main idea_	M	15
	Mark the statement that is _too broad_	B	5
	Mark the statement that is _too narrow_	N	5

a. Pythons squeeze their victims to death and devour them by dragging their jaws over them. ☐ _____

b. Pythons have teeth that are thin and delicate. ☐ _____

c. Pythons have unusual and interesting living habits. ☐ _____

Score 15 points for each correct answer.   **Score**

Subject Matter   **2**   This passage focuses on the
     ☐ a. python's size.
     ☐ b. most poisonous snakes.
     ☐ c. python's hunting method.
     ☐ d. snake family. _____

Supporting   **3**   The snake kills its prey
Details
     ☐ a. with poisonous venom.
     ☐ b. by biting it.
     ☐ c. by suffocating it.
     ☐ d. by swallowing it. _____

Conclusion   **4**   This passage does not imply that pythons
     ☐ a. eat many different kinds of animals.
     ☐ b. are strong.
     ☐ c. have an unusual mouth structure.
     ☐ d. are poisonous snakes. _____

Clarifying   **5**   The author gives the readers a good under-
Devices   standing of pythons through the use of
     ☐ a. metaphors.
     ☐ b. description.
     ☐ c. comparison.
     ☐ d. examples. _____

Vocabulary   **6**   <u>Hapless</u> in this passage means
in Context
     ☐ a. headless.
     ☐ b. hidden.
     ☐ c. unlucky.
     ☐ d. frightened. _____

Add your scores for questions 1–6. Enter the total here   **Total**
and on the graph on page 217.   **Score**   _____

46 Insects for Dinner

Most Americans seem to crave variety in their diets, judging by the popularity of foreign restaurants. But though many people would be willing to sample a curry dish from India, a real Hungarian goulash, or even Japanese sushi, very few would want to indulge in a kind of food that is popular in many countries: insects.

Eating insects actually is eminently sensible. There are certainly enough of them around, and though most are too small to bother with, many grow to a <u>respectable</u> size or live in dense groups that can be easily harvested. They are very nutritious: after all, many birds and mammals ingest diets consisting of nothing but insects. And since insects contain a fair amount of salt, they are already well seasoned. Indeed, in those countries where insects are eaten, they are usually considered great delicacies. The goliath beetle is a prize catch in Africa; caterpillars are a popular dish in Mexico, where they are fried and served under the name of "agave worms"; and chocolate-covered bees and ants are favorite candies in Switzerland.

It is unlikely that canned grasshoppers will become popular in America in the near future, but who knows? Perhaps in years to come people will rid themselves of their prejudice against insects and will find themselves going out to dig for grubs as eagerly as others now go out to gather mushrooms.

Main Idea   1

	Answer	Score
Mark the _main idea_	M	15
Mark the statement that is _too broad_	B	5
Mark the statement that is _too narrow_	N	5

a. Insects contain a fair amount of salt.	☐	_____
b. Many different creatures are edible.	☐	_____
c. Insects can be a good source of food.	☐	_____

Score 15 points for each correct answer.   **Score**

Subject Matter   **2**   The subject of this passage is
     ☐ a. how to open a restaurant.
     ☐ b. the behavior of primitive people.
     ☐ c. American shopping habits.
     ☐ d. the use of insects as food.   _____

Supporting Details   **3**   Agave worms are
     ☐ a. caterpillars found in Mexico.
     ☐ b. fried vegetables.
     ☐ c. pests found on agave trees.
     ☐ d. salty and very crunchy.   _____

Conclusion   **4**   This passage implies that insects are not a popular food in America because
     ☐ a. they can transmit deadly diseases.
     ☐ b. Americans don't like salty food.
     ☐ c. Americans don't like the idea of eating such creatures.
     ☐ d. very few restaurants offer them.   _____

Clarifying Devices   **5**   In developing the idea that insects are good to eat, the author uses
     ☐ a. an emotional appeal.
     ☐ b. several specific examples.
     ☐ c. the opinions of some famous people.
     ☐ d. only broad generalizations.   _____

Vocabulary in Context   **6**   In this passage <u>respectable</u> means
     ☐ a. awesome.
     ☐ b. well-behaved.
     ☐ c. fairly large.
     ☐ d. dangerous.   _____

Add your scores for questions 1–6. Enter the total here and on the graph on page 217.   **Total Score**   _____

47 The Exploits of Nellie Bly

Many people criticize today's newspapers as sensationalist, catering to the public's morbid curiosity. But journalism a century ago was just as notorious. Publishers of that era routinely competed with each other for wild, extravagant stories that could draw in the most readers. It was an ideal atmosphere for a daring reporter like Nellie Bly to thrive in.

Bly, whose real name was Elizabeth Corcoran, had to work to make her way in the world. Unlike many women of the time, however, she refused to let the working world intimidate her. Her first big opportunity as a reporter came in 1885 after she wrote an angry letter denouncing the Pittsburgh *Dispatch* for an article it had run criticizing women forced to work outside the home. The intrigued editor hired Bly for her "spirit," and soon she was investigating the situations of female factory workers. Bly cared less about their jobs than about their lives after work—their amusements, their motivations, their fears and aspirations. She produced an article totally unlike what other reporters of the time were writing: personal, insightful, *meaningful.*

By 1887 Bly had a job with the New York *World,* one of the leading papers of the day. She quickly became famous for undercover stories about women in a mental hospital. Soon she had investigated life as a maid, a chorus girl, even a prostitute. In her best-known exploit, in 1890, Bly beat the famous "around the world in 80 days" trip Jules Verne had described in his novel. Traveling by steamship, train, even ricksha, Bly reported from each stop. A spellbound nation hung on every word. Only 25, Bly had become an international celebrity.

Main Idea	1		Answer	Score
	Mark the *main idea*		M	15
	Mark the statement that is *too broad*		B	5
	Mark the statement that is *too narrow*		N	5

a. Journalism a hundred years ago was as sensational as journalism today. ☐ _____

b. Nellie Bly went around the word in fewer than 80 days. ☐ _____

c. Nellie Bly was a spirited reporter who investigated many situations to write good stories. ☐ _____

Subject Matter	2	This passage is mostly about
		☐ a. reporting practices in the late 1800s.
		☐ b. the life of Nellie Bly.
		☐ c. the career of Nellie Bly.
		☐ d. Nellie Bly and Jules Verne. _____

Supporting Details	3	Bly's first newspaper job was
		☐ a. with the New York *World.*
		☐ b. with the Pittsburgh *Dispatch.*
		☐ c. in the small town where she grew up.
		☐ d. as a reporter covering international crime. _____

Conclusion	4	Jules Verne's novel was
		☐ a. popular at the time.
		☐ b. about a woman reporter.
		☐ c. fiction based on fact.
		☐ d. too difficult for most people to read. _____

Clarifying Devices	5	The writer introduces this piece by using
		☐ a. a comparison.
		☐ b. a surprising quote.
		☐ c. a brief anecdote.
		☐ d. statistics. _____

Vocabulary in Context	6	<u>Denouncing</u> means
		☐ a. praising.
		☐ b. questioning.
		☐ c. informing on.
		☐ d. severely criticizing. _____

Add your scores for questions 1–6. Enter the total here and on the graph on page 217.   **Total Score** _____

48 Just a Coincidence?

From 1840 to 1960 every American president elected in the twentieth year—Harrison in 1840, Lincoln in 1860, Garfield in 1880, McKinley in 1900, Harding in 1920, Roosevelt in 1940, and Kennedy in 1960—died in office. Many writers have remarked on this coincidence, but the similarities between the lives of presidents Lincoln and Kennedy are particularly unusual.

Remarkably strong parallels can be observed between the careers of these two charismatic leaders. Lincoln was first elected to Congress in 1846, Kennedy in 1946. Both men had been in the armed forces, and each worked for the cause of civil rights. Both presidents were assassinated: Lincoln was killed by a man born in 1839 and Kennedy by one born in 1939. Both assassins were Southerners who themselves were killed before they could be tried.

Additionally, the assassinations both occurred on Fridays, with the wives of the presidents present. Lincoln had a secretary named Kennedy who warned him not to attend the theater on the night he was killed. President Kennedy's secretary, a Mrs. Lincoln, warned him against visiting Dallas, which came to be the site of his death. Southerners named Johnson—Andrew, born in 1808, and Lyndon, born in 1908—succeeded both Lincoln and Kennedy.

With more digging, no doubt, more of these similarities could be discovered. Are the similarities significant, or do people find coincidences where they look for them? Perhaps they do. At any rate, if John Kennedy had been aware of the remarkable parallels between his and Lincoln's life, might he have listened to his secretary and cancelled his fateful Dallas trip?

Main Idea	1		
		Answer	Score
	Mark the *main idea*	M	15
	Mark the statement that is *too broad*	B	5
	Mark the statement that is *too narrow*	N	5

a. There are amazing similarities in the details of the lives of many American presidents. ☐ _____

b. The circumstances of Lincoln's and Kennedy's deaths were very similar. ☐ _____

c. There are many striking parallels in the histories of Kennedy and Lincoln. ☐ _____

Score 15 points for each correct answer.   **Score**

Subject Matter   2   The best alternate title for this passage would be
- [ ] a. American Presidents.
- [ ] b. The Lincoln-Kennedy Assassinations.
- [ ] c. The Careers of Lincoln and Kennedy.
- [ ] d. Lincoln and Kennedy: Striking Similarities.   _____

Supporting Details   3   The secretaries of both Lincoln and Kennedy
- [ ] a. saw the assassinations.
- [ ] b. were named Johnson.
- [ ] c. advised them not to go to the places where they were killed.
- [ ] d. were born in years ending in 39.   _____

Conclusion   4   The writer seems to think that coincidences
- [ ] a. definitely have hidden meanings.
- [ ] b. may or may not occur simply by chance.
- [ ] c. are always found wherever people look for them.
- [ ] d. do not occur very often.   _____

Clarifying Devices   5   The first paragraph catches the reader's attention with a
- [ ] a. surprising fact.
- [ ] b. vivid adjective.
- [ ] c. first-hand story.
- [ ] d. broad generalization.   _____

Vocabulary in Context   6   As used in this passage, <u>succeeded</u> is closest in meaning to
- [ ] a. achieved.
- [ ] b. came before.
- [ ] c. broke away from.
- [ ] d. came after.   _____

Add your scores for questions 1–6. Enter the total here and on the graph on page 217.   **Total Score**   _____

49 Want to Buy the Brooklyn Bridge?

As a rule, practical jokers either get stupendous laughs or get themselves into stupendous trouble. The outcome of a practical joke depends a great deal on the patience and sense of humor of the victim. Sometimes, however, a practical joke can be so <u>outrageous</u> that the only people who see the humor in it are the practical jokers themselves.

For two practical jokers named Lozier and DeVoe, the latter case was certainly true. Both gentlemen were retired and living in New York in 1824. It was not long before these two restless men were getting all the excitement they could handle.

It is a known fact that the southern portion of the island of Manhattan is sinking slowly into the ocean because of the weight of the many large buildings there. The practical joke was to convince fellow New Yorkers that the only way to save the island was to turn it around so the higher northern portion would be in the south, and the lower southern portion would be in the north.

Full-page ads were placed in newspapers to recruit an army of construction workers. The ad also mentioned that a gigantic anchor had been ordered and was now available to keep the island from blowing out to sea during a storm once the island had been twisted around.

On the appointed day, hundreds of workers appeared for their first day of work. Fortunately for the practical jokers, they were nowhere to be found. Rumor had it that a sudden illness had sent Lozier and DeVoe on an indefinitely long trip to an unknown destination.

Main Idea 1

	Answer	Score
Mark the *main idea*	M	15
Mark the statement that is *too broad*	B	5
Mark the statement that is *too narrow*	N	5

a. Lozier and DeVoe convinced hundreds of New Yorkers that they should turn Manhattan around. ☐ _____

b. Practical jokes can fool many people. ☐ _____

c. The south end of the island of Manhattan is sinking. ☐ _____

Subject Matter   **2**   The subject of this passage is
- [ ] a. the island of Manhattan.
- [ ] b. the life of Lozier and DeVoe.
- [ ] c. a practical joke.
- [ ] d. the summer of 1824.

_____

Supporting Details   **3**   Lozier and DeVoe planned to save Manhattan's
- [ ] a. southern end.
- [ ] b. eastern end.
- [ ] c. northern end.
- [ ] d. western end.

_____

Conclusion   **4**   It is evident that Lozier and DeVoe
- [ ] a. were scientists.
- [ ] b. were not taken seriously.
- [ ] c. had unusual senses of humor.
- [ ] d. were construction engineers.

_____

Clarifying Devices   **5**   The writer treats the subject of the passage with
- [ ] a. deadly seriousness.
- [ ] b. obvious admiration.
- [ ] c. good humor.
- [ ] d. disapproval.

_____

Vocabulary in Context   **6**   Outrageous in this passage means
- [ ] a. cruel.
- [ ] b. filled with anger.
- [ ] c. fantastic.
- [ ] d. humorless.

_____

Add your scores for questions 1–6. Enter the total here and on the graph on page 217.   Total Score   _____

50 A Greek to Remember

Diogenes was a famous Greek philosopher of the fourth century B.C. who established the philosophy of cynicism. He often walked about in the daytime holding a lighted lantern, peering around as if he were looking for something. When questioned about his odd behavior he would reply, "I am searching for an honest man."

Diogenes <u>held</u> that a good person was self-sufficient and did not require material comforts or wealth. He believed that wealth and possessions constrained humanity's natural state of freedom. In keeping with this philosophy, Diogenes was perfectly satisfied with making his home in a large tub discarded from the temple of Cybele, the goddess of nature. This earthen tub, called a *pithos*, had formerly been used for holding wine or oil for sacrifices that were performed at the temple.

One day Alexander the Great, conqueror of half the civilized word, saw Diogenes sitting in his tub in the sunshine. So the king, surrounded by his courtiers, approached Diogenes and said, "I am Alexander the Great." The philosopher replied rather contemptuously, "I am Diogenes the Cynic." Alexander then asked him if he could help him in any way. "Yes," shot back Diogenes, "don't stand between me and the sun." A surprised Alexander then replied quickly, "If I were not Alexander, I would be Diogenes."

Main Idea	1		
		Answer	**Score**
	Mark the *main idea*	M	15
	Mark the statement that is *too broad*	B	5
	Mark the statement that is *too narrow*	N	5
	a. Diogenes was a Greek philosopher.	☐	_____
	b. Diogenes believed in humanity's natural state of freedom, a state without material luxuries.	☐	_____
	c. Diogenes was a famous Greek who strictly adhered to his philosophy of cynicism.	☐	_____

Subject Matter   **2**   This passage is mainly about
- ☐ a. cynical behavior.
- ☐ b. a famous cynic.
- ☐ c. ancient philosophers.
- ☐ d. Alexander the Great.   _____

Supporting Details   **3**   According to Diogenes, material luxuries
- ☐ a. make people self-sufficient and independent.
- ☐ b. enslave people to a world of possessions.
- ☐ c. give people happiness and joy.
- ☐ d. cause people grief and pain.   _____

Conclusion   **4**   One can conclude that Diogenes's reply
- ☐ a. angered Alexander.
- ☐ b. confused Alexander.
- ☐ c. impressed Alexander.
- ☐ d. amazed Alexander.   _____

Clarifying Devices   **5**   The writer shows that Diogenes lived according to his beliefs by
- ☐ a. giving examples of things he did.
- ☐ b. using logical reasoning.
- ☐ c. comparing his life with the lives of other philosophers.
- ☐ d. contrasting his lifestyle with Alexander's.   _____

Vocabulary in Context   **6**   <u>Held</u> in this passage means
- ☐ a. confirmed.
- ☐ b. refuted.
- ☐ c. believed.
- ☐ d. opposed.   _____

Add your scores for questions 1–6. Enter the total here and on the graph on page 217.   **Total Score**   _____

51 The Story of the Hamburger

It would be hard to find a person in America who has never eaten a hamburger, but this popular food was not originally made in America. The original hamburger can be traced back to the Middle Ages, when Russians ate raw meat that was scraped and shredded with a dull knife and formed into patties. It was called Tartar steak. This was the first step in a long series of developments that eventually resulted in hamburger as we know it today.

German sailors picked up the raw meat delicacy in their contacts with Russians and brought it back to their home port of Hamburg. But the people there were unused to eating raw meat, so they broiled the outside of the Russian steak; thus the hamburg steak was born.

The hamburg steak was brought to America in the nineteenth century by German immigrants. Louis Lassen, a cook in New Haven, Connecticut, modified the hamburg steak by sandwiching it between two pieces of bread. But the true American hamburger came into existence in St. Louis at the Louisiana Purchase Exposition in 1904. A harried cook at the fair quickly slapped broiled beef patties between buns and served them to a demanding crowd, which gulped them down joyously.

At first this new food creation was made from scraps of poorer cuts of meat that were not used for anything else, but before long scraps were not enough. The demand for greater quantities of hamburger could only be met by using more and better cuts. Hamburger stands sprang up all over the country, and a side industry of condiments, such as ketchup and relish, grew up and prospered along with the popular hamburger.

Main Idea	1		
		Answer	Score
Mark the *main idea*		**M**	15
Mark the statement that is *too broad*		**B**	5
Mark the statement that is *too narrow*		**N**	5
a. The hamburger is a popular food.		☐	_____
b. The history of the hamburger is a very long one.		☐	_____
c. German sailors brought shredded meat home to Hamburg from Russia.		☐	_____

Subject Matter   **2**   Another good title for this passage would be
- ☐ a. The St. Louis Fair.
- ☐ b. Russian Eating Habits.
- ☐ c. The Development of the Hamburger.
- ☐ d. The First Hamburger Stand.

_____

Supporting Details   **3**   The hamburg steak was first introduced in America by
- ☐ a. Russian soldiers.
- ☐ b. German immigrants.
- ☐ c. a St. Louis cook.
- ☐ d. foreign sailors.

_____

Conclusion   **4**   We can assume that the citizens of Hamburg
- ☐ a. liked only fresh raw meat.
- ☐ b. thought the Russians very clever.
- ☐ c. were slow in taking on new customs.
- ☐ d. found raw meat unappetizing.

_____

Clarifying Devices   **5**   The writer talks about the emergence of the hamburger by
- ☐ a. retelling Russian folk tales.
- ☐ b. describing eyewitness accounts.
- ☐ c. describing the changes step by step.
- ☐ d. showing that other foods changed too.

_____

Vocabulary in Context   **6**   Harried here means
- ☐ a. busy.
- ☐ b. careless.
- ☐ c. lazy.
- ☐ d. sloppy.

_____

Add your scores for questions 1–6. Enter the total here and on the graph on page 217.   **Total Score**

_____

52 What an Actor!

There isn't much likelihood of an uneducated, untrained man being hired to do three very different, highly professional jobs in his life. But a man named Ferdinand Waldo Demera accomplished just that. He was such a <u>consummate</u> actor that he wrote his own roles and played them out upon life's broad stage.

Demera realized early that the only way he could succeed in life would be by using his special powers of deceit. To convince people of his qualifications, Demera forged signatures on an impressive array of references. Then his confident manner and convincing acting made him a success at almost everything he tried. As a surgeon on a Royal Canadian ship during the Korean War, Demera performed 19 successful operations—and he had had no medical training.

Later, acting as a college professor in applied psychology, he was well liked and admired by both students and faculty. But the day came when Demera's charade was uncovered, so he was forced to keep a low profile for several years. Then he obtained a position as a guidance counselor in a prison. True to form, Demera turned in a very good performance and actually helped many of the inmates.

Demera's trickery eventually became well known, and the story of his highly successful "acting" career was written. Hollywood bought the story and made it into a movie. It was rumored that Demera applied for the lead in his own life's story, but, ironically, he did not pass the screen test. It was the first time he failed to fool.

Main Idea 1

	Answer	Score
Mark the *main idea*	M	15
Mark the statement that is *too broad*	B	5
Mark the statement that is *too narrow*	N	5

a. Demera's life story was made into a movie. ☐ _____

b. Some people are very good actors and can fake their way through life. ☐ _____

c. Demera fooled people into believing that he was trained for a variety of high-level jobs. ☐ _____

Score 15 points for each correct answer.   Score

Subject Matter   2 This passage describes
- ☐ a. a life of crime.
- ☐ b. the life of Ferdinand Demera.
- ☐ c. a professional Hollywood actor.
- ☐ d. the talents required for acting.

_____

Supporting Details   3 As a naval surgeon, Demera
- ☐ a. performed admirably.
- ☐ b. disgraced himself.
- ☐ c. performed no operations.
- ☐ d. was caught and discharged.

_____

Conclusion   4 This passage suggests that Demera might have been an excellent
- ☐ a. writer.
- ☐ b. military leader.
- ☐ c. card player.
- ☐ d. actor.

_____

Clarifying Devices   5 A person who keeps a "low profile"
- ☐ a. refuses to speak.
- ☐ b. wears unattractive clothing.
- ☐ c. hides from the law.
- ☐ d. avoids drawing public attention.

_____

Vocabulary in Context   6 Consummate is synonymous with
- ☐ a. reasonable.
- ☐ b. skilled.
- ☐ c. experienced.
- ☐ d. old.

_____

Add your scores for questions 1–6. Enter the total here and on the graph on page 217.   Total Score

_____

53 A Mystery Solved

During the 1950s Peter Glob, a Danish archaeologist, was responsible for unraveling the mystery of a centuries-old murder.

Several well-preserved, naked male bodies were discovered in Danish peat bogs. Upon examining these bodies, Glob found that they dated back to Denmark's Iron Age, more than 1,600 years ago. The apparent fact that the men had died violently, by hanging or throat slitting, was the first clue to intrigue Glob. Several victims wore twisted hide thongs around their necks, and their hands and feet were soft, indicating that they had never done heavy labor. Autopsies revealed that the men's last meal consisted of grains and seeds. Glob found the absence of meat puzzling, because during the Iron Age people were not vegetarians.

In search of further information, Glob turned to the writings of Tacitus, the ancient Roman historian who had written about the tribes of northwest Europe. Tacitus described rites of human sacrifice that were made to the Earth Goddess. The ancient tribes held these rites in early spring, to guarantee the fertility of their fields. From this information, Glob deduced that the dead men were priests or men of high rank, which would account for their soft hands, and that the victims had been fed a ritual meal of plant seeds before they were sacrificed. Glob further deduced that the victims' leather neck thongs represented the metal ring that Tacitus had described as being a symbol for the Earth Goddess. Glob concluded that these bog men had been sacrificed to the very thing that preserved them—Mother Earth.

Main Idea	1		
		Answer	Score
	Mark the *main idea*	M	15
	Mark the statement that is *too broad*	B	5
	Mark the statement that is *too narrow*	N	5

a. The preserved bodies had soft hands and feet. ☐ _____

b. A Danish archaeologist solved the mystery of the men in the bog. ☐ _____

c. Archaeologists uncover many mysterious things in the course of their work. ☐ _____

Subject Matter	2	Which would be the best alternate title for this passage?

    ☐ a. Tribes of Northwest Europe
    ☐ b. Peter Glob, Danish Archaeologist
    ☐ c. Identifying the Bodies in the Bog
    ☐ d. Murder in Ancient Europe   _____

Supporting Details   **3** According to the passage, the dead men's bodies were
    ☐ a. decomposed.
    ☐ b. tied together.
    ☐ c. well-preserved.
    ☐ d. cut into pieces.   _____

Conclusion   **4** We can conclude from the passage that the key information linking the men in the bog to ancient human sacrifices was provided by
    ☐ a. autopsies of the bodies.
    ☐ b. the writings of Tacitus.
    ☐ c. the examination of the victim's hands and feet.
    ☐ d. the positions of the bodies.   _____

Clarifying Devices   **5** The writer's purpose in the first sentence is to
    ☐ a. mislead the reader.
    ☐ b. provide important information.
    ☐ c. arouse the reader's interest.
    ☐ d. scare the reader.   _____

Vocabulary in Context   **6** As used in the passage, the word <u>intrigue</u> means
    ☐ a. maneuver.
    ☐ b. frighten.
    ☐ c. greatly interest.
    ☐ d. mislead.   _____

Add your scores for questions 1–6. Enter the total here and on the graph on page 217.   **Total Score**   _____

54 Stylish Living?

The royal palace at Versailles, the center of court life during the reign of Louis XIV, is today a symbol of dazzling beauty and <u>opulent</u> living. Millions of gold francs were spent in building and furnishing its lavish chambers, halls, and gardens. So it is difficult to imagine the royal palace as it was in its heyday—cold, crowded, and filthy.

The chimneys in Versailles Palace were so wide that fires were easily extinguished by rain or snow, and wind blew smoke back into the chambers. Heating the enormous rooms was impossible, so ladies who wore fashionably low-cut dresses suffered for style.

Louis XIV enlarged the palace greatly, but because he preferred to have his nobles near him, the vast estate still swarmed with courtiers, sometimes as many as 10,000. He also favored giving the populace the opportunity to observe their sovereign at home. Sightseers were allowed to troop through the staterooms and gaze upon the king as he dined.

The hallways were as private as city streets. They were filled with vendors, tradesmen, and beggars. Cows and goats were brought to the doors of the chambers to be milked. Because there were no bathroom facilities, animal and human filth frequently piled up in the passageways of the palace.

With thousands of courtiers living closely together, with halls crowded with vendors and gawking townspeople, with courtyards filled with animals, and with filth everywhere, it is hard to imagine this royal palace as a fitting place for lavish and elegant living.

Main Idea	1		
		Answer	**Score**
	Mark the *main idea*	M	15
	Mark the statement that is *too broad*	B	5
	Mark the statement that is *too narrow*	N	5

a. At its height, the magnificent palace of Versailles was actually an unpleasant place to live. ☐ _____

b. Versailles was very unsanitary due to overcrowding with people and animals. ☐ _____

c. Life in palaces of the past was less glorious than most people think. ☐ _____

Subject Matter   **2**   The passage focuses on the
☐ a. reign of Louis XIV.
☐ b. construction of Versailles.
☐ c. discomforts of Versailles.
☐ d. beauty of Versailles.   _____

Supporting Details   **3**   According to the passage, Louis XIV believed in
☐ a. maintaining large gardens.
☐ b. keeping the palace cold.
☐ c. the need for a quiet retreat.
☐ d. allowing people to view their king.   _____

Conclusion   **4**   At Versailles, during the reign of Louis XIV, you would **not** have expected to find
☐ a. fine paintings and statues.
☐ b. comfortable living quarters.
☐ c. government officials and nobles.
☐ d. peasants and vendors.   _____

Clarifying Devices   **5**   In developing the main idea, the writer relies mostly on
☐ a. quotations.
☐ b. picturesque language.
☐ c. emotion.
☐ d. description.   _____

Vocabulary in Context   **6**   As used in the passage, opulent means
☐ a. rich.
☐ b. middle-class.
☐ c. isolated.
☐ d. comfortable.   _____

Add your scores for questions 1–6. Enter the total here and on the graph on page 217.   **Total Score**   _____

55 Hurricanes

They occur with <u>monotonous</u> regularity every year, usually commencing in August and fading away in early November. They have names like Fran and Bonnie and Andrew and Camille—friendly, everyday sorts of names. But these gigantic, often monstrous storms—hurricanes—are the farthest thing from friendly, as anyone who has endured the fury of one will attest.

Though *typhoon* and *cyclone* are essentially synonyms describing the same formations, the word *hurricane* refers only to violent wind-and-rain-filled storms that develop over the western Atlantic and strike North America and the Caribbean. A storm becomes a hurricane only if its winds exceed 72 miles per hour; however, the worst hurricanes may be twice that strong.

Warm ocean waters and low atmospheric pressure are essential conditions for hurricanes. Low pressure—when the atmosphere does not bear down too hard on the earth—pulls warm air up from the water's surface; the lower the pressure in an area, the more air that will enter it and rise. In fact, the low-pressure area functions as a chimney: the warm air ascends, cools, condenses into rain, and spreads, forming a thunderstorm that gets larger as more air is drawn in.

At the hurricane's center is the eye, an area of intensely low pressure where, surprisingly, the air is calm and the sky is clear. Around this eye, however, winds are raging—blowing in one direction on one side and in the opposite direction on the other. Property may be destroyed by the sheer velocity of the winds, by the terrible flooding they provoke as they raise the ocean's waters and those of nearby rivers to abnormally high levels, or, in the worst cases, by both.

Main Idea	1	Answer	Score
	Mark the *main idea*	M	15
	Mark the statement that is *too broad*	B	5
	Mark the statement that is *too narrow*	N	5

a. Typhoons and cyclones are formed in the same way as hurricanes. ☐ ____

b. Hurricanes are violent storms formed in certain areas and possessing specific characteristics. ☐ ____

c. Any storm with very high winds can cause great damage. ☐ ____

Subject Matter   **2**   The subject of this passage is
☐ a. how hurricanes develop and what they do.
☐ b. why hurricanes are given names.
☐ c. why tropical storms are dangerous.
☐ d. why the eye of a hurricane forms as it does.   _____

Supporting Details   **3**   Conditions needed for a hurricane to form are
☐ a. high pressure and rain.
☐ b. low pressure and warm ocean waters.
☐ c. warm ocean waters and a clear sky.
☐ d. low pressure quickly changing to high pressure.   _____

Conclusion   **4**   Hurricanes usually cause
☐ a. water levels in the ocean and nearby rivers to get very high.
☐ b. the ocean waters to become cool.
☐ c. sharks and dolphins to flee an area.
☐ d. winds to blow mostly in one direction.   _____

Clarifying Devices   **5**   The author makes a comparison to a chimney in order to
☐ a. describe the heat of the water.
☐ b. paint a vivid word picture.
☐ c. show how a hurricane affects even well-built houses.
☐ d. show how warm air rises.   _____

Vocabulary in Context   **6**   In this passage <u>monotonous</u> means
☐ a. surprisingly tame.
☐ b. boringly similar.
☐ c. easily confused.
☐ d. barely known.   _____

Add your scores for questions 1–6. Enter the total here and on the graph on page 217.   **Total Score**   _____

56 Maker of Great Violins

Hundreds of violins are made every day. However, the finest and most sought-after violins were handcrafted by an Italian violin maker over 250 years ago. The craftsman's name was Antonius Stradivarius, and any one of his violins is worth over $100,000 today.

Stradivarius, who was born in 1644, began his career as a violin maker's apprentice. Working on his own by 1680, he became determined to make instruments that could reproduce tones as <u>rich</u> as those produced by the human voice. He tested several shapes and styles for his violins until he arrived at a design that pleased him. During his career he crafted over 1,100 violins. Those still in existence have become treasured possessions.

Unfortunately, the secret of the Stradivarius violin died with its maker. During his lifetime Stradivarius kept his notes safely hidden; even his two sons, who helped him in his workshop, did not know all the steps involved in each violin's construction.

Through the years, many experts have offered possible explanations for the unique tone of a "Strad." Some say it is the instrument's shape and the harmony of its parts. Others suggest that the secret lies in the special properties of the wood, which Stradivarius obtained from native Italian trees that no longer exist. The most widely accepted supposition is that the exquisite tone of the violins is created by the varnish that the old master used to coat his instruments. Chemists have analyzed and reproduced, as closely as possible, the varnish, and its application has improved the sound of many violins. Still, no violin maker has been able to fully reproduce the tone of Stradivarius's violins.

Main Idea 1

	Answer	Score
Mark the *main idea*	M	15
Mark the statement that is *too broad*	B	5
Mark the statement that is *too narrow*	N	5

a. Stradivarius crafted the world's finest violins. ☐ _____

b. Stradivarius was an Italian violin maker. ☐ _____

c. Stradivarius was an extremely talented craftsman. ☐ _____

Score 15 points for each correct answer.   Score

Subject Matter   2   Another good title for this passage would be
- [ ] a. How to Make Violins.
- [ ] b. Expensive Violins.
- [ ] c. What Was Stradivarius's Secret?
- [ ] d. Italian Violin Makers.

_____

Supporting Details   3   According to this passage, Stradivarius made
- [ ] a. hundreds of violins every day.
- [ ] b. over 100,000 violins during his career.
- [ ] c. only one violin.
- [ ] d. hundreds of violins during his career.

_____

Conclusion   4   We can conclude from the passage that Stradivarius's
- [ ] a. notes were found by chemists.
- [ ] b. notes were never found.
- [ ] c. secrets were learned when he was an apprentice.
- [ ] d. notes were left to his sons.

_____

Clarifying Devices   5   The writer shows the uniqueness of Stradivarius's violins by stating that
- [ ] a. Stradivarius made only 1,100 violins.
- [ ] b. all of Stradivarius's violins were varnished.
- [ ] c. Stradivarius experimented with different styles.
- [ ] d. no one has been able to duplicate their sound.

_____

Vocabulary in Context   6   In this passage the word <u>rich</u> means
- [ ] a. wealthy.
- [ ] b. highly amusing.
- [ ] c. full and mellow.
- [ ] d. producing or yielding abundantly.

_____

Add your scores for questions 1–6. Enter the total here and on the graph on page 217.   Total Score

_____

57 A Mysterious Island

If mysteries fascinate you, you might try looking into the one surrounding Easter Island, which lies in the South Pacific. Ever since the Dutch explorer Jakob Roggeveen discovered the small, isolated island in 1722, experts have remained perplexed as to the origin of the strange artifacts found there.

Roggeveen found the extinct volcanoes on the island interesting, but he was most astonished by the more than 600 huge statues on the island. The statues were almost identical, each carved in the shape of a human head approximately 40 feet high and weighing about 50 tons. All the heads gazed sternly out to sea. The figures were carved from a type of volcanic rock called *tufa*.

Roggeveen later found the quarry where the tufa was mined. He also discovered 150 more partially finished statues and evidence that seemed to suggest that their sculptors had, for some unknown reason, stopped working rather suddenly.

Many questions remain concerning the strange stone heads of Easter Island. Contemporary archaeologists who have investigated the site have uncovered more questions than answers. Many of the statues were discovered to have bodies buried deep in the ground. The reason for this is unknown. Archaeologists have also puzzled over how the enormous stone figures were moved up to ten miles from their original construction sites—a seemingly impossible task, because the island has few trees that could be used as rollers. Further investigations may someday yield the answers to the mysterious questions surrounding Easter Island. But it is just as possible that the mystery will remain forever unsolved.

Main Idea 1

	Answer	Score
Mark the *main idea*	M	15
Mark the statement that is *too broad*	B	5
Mark the statement that is *too narrow*	N	5

a. Easter Island contains many mysteries. ☐ ____

b. Easter Island contains huge stone figures whose origins have remained a mystery. ☐ ____

c. Easter Island contains over 600 stone statues. ☐ ____

Subject Matter   **2**   Another good title for this passage might be
- ☐ a. The Life of Dutch Explorer Jakob Roggeveen.
- ☐ b. Statues of Easter Island.
- ☐ c. Archaeological Expeditions in the South Pacific.
- ☐ d. Island of the Aliens.   _____

Supporting Details   **3**   The statues were carved from
- ☐ a. limestone.
- ☐ b. marble.
- ☐ c. granite.
- ☐ d. tufa.   _____

Conclusion   **4**   The origin of the statues of Easter Island
- ☐ a. is known to be alien.
- ☐ b. can be explained by archaeologists.
- ☐ c. is not worth worrying about.
- ☐ d. is still a mystery.   _____

Clarifying Devices   **5**   This story is presented
- ☐ a. in reverse order of events.
- ☐ b. as a logical argument.
- ☐ c. through questions and answers.
- ☐ d. in time sequence.   _____

Vocabulary in Context   **6**   In this passage <u>contemporary</u> means
- ☐ a. modern-day.
- ☐ b. stylish.
- ☐ c. doubtful.
- ☐ d. concerned.   _____

Add your scores for questions 1–6. Enter the total here and on the graph on page 217.   **Total Score**   _____

58 An Ingenious Solution

In the era before the arrival of the white settlers, Native Americans managed to survive and prosper without any of the inventions of more technologically advanced societies. In fact, some of their accomplishments almost defy explanation. The native people depended heavily on timber for their existence, but how was it that they could cut down trees without the aid of iron axes—indeed, without any metal tools at all?

Native Americans solved that problem as they did other problems that confronted them in their wilderness environment—by using good old-fashioned American ingenuity. The hardest material available to the American Indians was stone, while the most powerful force they possessed was fire. By combining these two tools, they were able to <u>fell</u> trees quite efficiently.

The American Indians made stone hatchets. These were sharpened in preparation for each timber harvest. For a harvest, they first selected the trees to be felled. Then they would build a fire to encircle the bottom of a tree. The flames would burn the trunk in a narrow circular ring near the bottom of the tree. The charred wood could be easily hacked away with a stone axe. When the first charred layer had been cut away, another layer was charred and hacked away, and this procedure was repeated until the tree toppled.

Stone and fire proved to be adequate substitutes for metals, which Native Americans of this early time never knew existed.

Main Idea	1		
		Answer	Score
	Mark the *main idea*	M	15
	Mark the statement that is *too broad*	B	5
	Mark the statement that is *too narrow*	N	5

   a. Native Americans relied on trees for their existence. ☐ _____

   b. Fire was used to fell trees. ☐ _____

   c. Native Americans used great ingenuity to cut down trees. ☐ _____

Score 15 points for each correct answer. **Score**

Subject Matter 2 The focus of this passage is
☐ a. how Native Americans built fires.
☐ b. how Native Americans discovered iron.
☐ c. how Native Americans felled trees.
☐ d. Native Americans and their customs.
_____

Supporting Details 3 Felling trees was accomplished mainly with the aid of
☐ a. fire and vines used as rope.
☐ b. stone and fire.
☐ c. nature.
☐ d. patience.
_____

Conclusion 4 For American Indians, felling trees was a
☐ a. job.
☐ b. hobby.
☐ c. sport.
☐ d. custom.
_____

Clarifying Devices 5 The author reveals Native Americans' ingenuity with
☐ a. a short story.
☐ b. a humorous anecdote.
☐ c. a documented incident.
☐ d. a description of a process.
_____

Vocabulary in Context 6 In this passage the word <u>fell</u> means
☐ a. cruel.
☐ b. tripped.
☐ c. to cut down.
☐ d. the hide of an animal.
_____

Add your scores for questions 1–6. Enter the total here and on the graph on page 217. **Total Score** _____

59 Funeral for a Fly

You've undoubtedly heard that some people have funerals for their pets. Usually these funerals are for animals that have been true and loyal companions. Thus you might be surprised to hear that the brilliant Roman poet Virgil, who lived from 70 to 19 B.C., actually had a funeral for his pet fly. But there was a reason for this strange occurrence.

When the second triumvirate came into power in Rome, in 43 B.C., the three leaders—Augustus, Marc Antony, and Lepidus—enacted a law that transferred portions of land from the rich to the poorer war veterans. There were only a few exceptions, and among those parcels of land exempted from the decree were mausoleums.

Virgil, on hearing that his own villa might be slated for confiscation as well, devised a plan to save his property. He arranged a funeral and <u>subsequent</u> burial for a fly, pretending it was a much-loved pet. The burial took place as part of a lavish ceremony, amid much pomp and circumstance. The ceremony featured speeches by a number of prominent Romans, including Virgil himself, bereaving the loss of the fly. The cost of this elaborate affair came to over $150,000 in today's currency.

As a result of the ruse, after the ceremony Virgil's house was considered a mausoleum and was exempted from the provisions of the ordinance.

Main Idea	1	Answer	Score
	Mark the *main idea*	M	15
	Mark the statement that is *too broad*	B	5
	Mark the statement that is *too narrow*	N	5

a. Virgil devised an elaborate funeral ceremony. ☐ _____

b. Virgil found a way to avoid losing his property. ☐ _____

c. To avoid losing land, Virgil devised an elaborate burial ceremony for a fly. ☐ _____

Score 15 points for each correct answer. **Score**

Subject Matter **2** This passage is about
- ☐ a. Roman politics in the first century B.C.
- ☐ b. an expensive legal loophole.
- ☐ c. Virgil's pet fly.
- ☐ d. Roman burial customs.

_____

Supporting Details **3** The lands of the rich were to be confiscated in order to
- ☐ a. give poor farmers more land.
- ☐ b. increase taxes for the state.
- ☐ c. provide war veterans with land.
- ☐ d. divide the land more evenly among the city dwellers.

_____

Conclusion **4** One can conclude from the passage that
- ☐ a. Virgil didn't really love the fly.
- ☐ b. Virgil didn't really bury a fly.
- ☐ c. flies were common pets in Roman households.
- ☐ d. the graves of pets were not considered exempt from the ordinance.

_____

Clarifying Devices **5** The information in the second paragraph is necessary to the story because it
- ☐ a. adds interesting historical background.
- ☐ b. gives relevant information necessary to the story.
- ☐ c. serves as an expanding element in story development.
- ☐ d. is a smooth transition from the first to the third paragraph.

_____

Vocabulary in Context **6** <u>Subsequent</u> means
- ☐ a. contemporary.
- ☐ b. simultaneous.
- ☐ c. following.
- ☐ d. extemporaneous.

_____

Add your scores for questions 1–6. Enter the total here and on the graph on page 217. **Total Score**

_____

60 The Telltale Beam

If you have ever seen the classic film *Raiders of the Lost Ark* you will remember the small opening in the roof of a tomb that allowed a beam of sunlight to strike a spot on the tomb's floor at a certain time each day. Well, there is a similar device in a real cathedral in Italy, although its purpose is not quite as exciting as the one in the film.

In 1420, 72 years before Columbus discovered America, a great Italian architect named Filippo Brunelleschi built a cathedral in the city of Florence. He left a small opening in the dome, which allowed a slender beam of sunlight to shine through onto the church floor. Built into the floor was a small metal plate. Every year, on the twenty-first of June, the beam of sunlight was supposed to fall on this metal plate—and that it has done, every year without fail for over 575 years!

Why was the cathedral designed with this special <u>feature</u>? Well, the church was built in a place that was marshy, which means that the ground was very unstable, like mud. If it ever happened that the light beam did not strike the special metal plate on June 21, it would mean that the church had shifted, or moved out of place, on its base. People would know that they had to fix the cathedral so it wouldn't fall or they would have time to make sure everyone nearby was safe in case it collapsed.

Main Idea	1		
		Answer	**Score**
	Mark the *main idea*	M	15
	Mark the statement that is *too broad*	B	5
	Mark the statement that is *too narrow*	N	5

a. Brunelleschi built the cathedral on marshy ground.

b. One must be careful when building cathedrals.

c. The cathedral was designed with a special feature that warned if the building shifted.

Score 15 points for each correct answer.   **Score**

Subject Matter   **2**   This passage deals mostly with
- ☐ a. *Raiders of the Lost Ark.*
- ☐ b. a famous Italian architect.
- ☐ c. a cathedral in Florence.
- ☐ d. metal floor plates.

                        _____

Supporting Details   **3**   The special device was added because
- ☐ a. the church might fall in an earthquake.
- ☐ b. it could warn people if the cathedral had moved.
- ☐ c. the rest of the cathedral floor was mud.
- ☐ d. it made the cathedral more stable.

                        _____

Conclusion   **4**   You can **not** conclude from this story that
- ☐ a. the cathedral is still standing today.
- ☐ b. the sun falls on the metal plate only once a year.
- ☐ c. Brunelleschi grew rich from his idea.
- ☐ d. it is dangerous to build on unstable ground.

                        _____

Clarifying Devices   **5**   The writer mentions Columbus to
- ☐ a. tell of another famous Italian.
- ☐ b. make the story more exciting.
- ☐ c. point out the difference in achievements of the two men.
- ☐ d. give an idea of the length of time since the event.

                        _____

Vocabulary in Context   **6**   In this passage <u>feature</u> means
- ☐ a. detail.
- ☐ b. main attraction.
- ☐ c. flaw.
- ☐ d. drawing.

                        _____

Add your scores for questions 1–6. Enter the total here and on the graph on page 217.   **Total Score**   _____

61 Blowing Their Tops

The eruption of Washington State's Mount St. Helens in 1980 caught Americans' attention because it occurred in their own country. But the Mount St. Helens cataclysm was only one in a long line of spectacular volcanic eruptions that have occurred over the past hundred years, many resulting in far more damage and loss of life.

In 1902 Mount Pelee in Martinique exploded, shooting out a huge cloud of burning gas and ashes that killed the 30,000 citizens of St. Pierre. An 1883 eruption that blew the top off the island of Krakatoa, near Sumatra, created a tidal wave that killed 36,000 people and spewed enough debris into the atmosphere to create a worldwide haze. When Mount Bezumyannaya erupted in Siberia in 1956, it spit out 2.4 billion tons of rock—enough debris to bury the city of Paris. Although its ashes were carried over 250 miles, no one was killed because the volcano was in a <u>remote</u> area. But the eruption of Nevado del Ruiz in Colombia in 1985 caused mudslides that resulted in the deaths of over 23,000 people.

In February of 1943, near the Mexican village of Paricutin, a man watched a volcano emerge in his cornfield. Dionisio Pulido was working in his field when a small crack in the ground began to expand and the earth started to shake. The stunned farmer watched until the danger forced him to leave. Out of the rift poured a cloud of smoke and sparks so large that at night it created a fireworks display visible for over 50 miles. By late March, the cloud had grown to a 20,000-foot column of smoke that was raining ashes on Mexico City, 200 miles away. Before the newborn volcano finally subsided, in 1952, it had created a mountain 1,200 feet high where Pulido's cornfield had been.

Main Idea	1		
		Answer	Score
Mark the *main idea*		M	15
Mark the statement that is *too broad*		B	5
Mark the statement that is *too narrow*		N	5

a. Many destructive volcanoes have erupted over the past hundred years. ☐ _____

b. In Mexico, a volcano sprang up in a farmer's cornfield. ☐ _____

c. Erupting volcanoes can destroy land and kill people. ☐ _____

Score 15 points for each correct answer.   **Score**

Subject Matter   **2**   The passage is primarily about
☐ a. great disasters.
☐ b. volcanic eruptions.
☐ c. Mount St. Helens.
☐ d. a volcano in Mexico.   _____

Supporting Details   **3**   According to the passage, Mount Bezumyannaya in Siberia
☐ a. emerged in a cornfield.
☐ b. caused a tidal wave.
☐ c. killed 36,000 people.
☐ d. killed no one.   _____

Conclusion   **4**   We can conclude from the passage that volcanoes
☐ a. do not occur anymore.
☐ b. occur in many different parts of the world.
☐ c. are really not terribly dangerous.
☐ d. usually erupt in the winter.   _____

Clarifying Devices   **5**   The story of the volcano in the cornfield is presented to demonstrate the fact that volcanoes
☐ a. kill a lot of people.
☐ b. erupt in Mexico.
☐ c. spring up from level ground.
☐ d. have often been unpredictable.   _____

Vocabulary in Context   **6**   In this passage <u>remote</u> is closest in meaning to
☐ a. isolated.
☐ b. lonely.
☐ c. rural.
☐ d. barren.   _____

Add your scores for questions 1–6. Enter the total here and on the graph on page 218.   **Total Score**   _____

123

62 His Final Escape

Many accounts have circulated concerning the death of renowned magician and escape artist Harry Houdini. The true story is an interesting but tragic one.

Houdini suffered an ankle injury in October of 1926. On the 22nd day of that fateful month, he was relaxing in his dressing room at the Princess Theatre in Montreal, the injured foot stretched out before him, when he was visited by a young student from McGill University. The student had previously done a sketch of Houdini and, having been invited to meet him again, decided to bring two of his friends along. One of them, an amateur boxer named Joselyn Gordon Whitehead, asked Houdini whether he could truly withstand any punch to the belly without flinching, as he had once <u>asserted</u>. Houdini apparently nodded somewhat absent-mindedly, not expecting what followed. Whitehead leaned down and struck him in the abdomen with great force. It is uncertain how many blows were delivered. Houdini gasped and explained that it was necessary to tighten the abdominal muscles before being struck.

Houdini didn't notice any immediate problem after this incident, but during his performance on the following Saturday he felt feverish and weak. He broke down on stage the next Monday and was immediately given a medical examination. It was discovered that he had suffered a ruptured appendix. Worse, peritonitis, an inflammation of the intestine, had set in. At that time the disease was always fatal, since drugs to combat it had not yet been developed. Although he fought the inevitable, in typical fashion, for about a week, he finally died on October 31, 1926. He was buried in the family plot in a cemetery in Queens, New York.

Main Idea	1		Answer	Score
	Mark the *main idea*		M	15
	Mark the statement that is *too broad*		B	5
	Mark the statement that is *too narrow*		N	5

a. Harry Houdini's death was caused by the actions of a careless student. ☐ _____

b. It is dangerous to act rashly. ☐ _____

c. Harry Houdini contracted peritonitis and died. ☐ _____

Subject Matter   **2**   This passage deals mainly with
- ☐ a. the quality of medicine in the 1920s.
- ☐ b. Houdini's success on stage.
- ☐ c. the death of a famous magician.
- ☐ d. a student's carelessness.

_____

Supporting Details   **3**   The McGill University student visited Houdini a second time because he
- ☐ a. wanted an autograph.
- ☐ b. wanted to bring a classmate.
- ☐ c. wanted to make a sketch.
- ☐ d. had been invited.

_____

Conclusion   **4**   Harry Houdini died of
- ☐ a. a complication from a broken ankle.
- ☐ b. a ruptured appendix.
- ☐ c. peritonitis, an inflammation of the intestine.
- ☐ d. a breakdown during a performance.

_____

Clarifying Devices   **5**   The purpose of the first paragraph is to
- ☐ a. provide interesting information as a lead-in.
- ☐ b. make a point about the frequency of rumors concerning celebrities.
- ☐ c. provide details necessary to understanding the story.
- ☐ d. make the account more believable.

_____

Vocabulary in Context   **6**   <u>Asserted</u> means
- ☐ a. claimed.
- ☐ b. questioned.
- ☐ c. demanded.
- ☐ d. suggested.

_____

Add your scores for questions 1–6. Enter the total here and on the graph on page 218.   **Total Score**

_____

63 Making Money

How easy has it been to produce counterfeit American currency? Much easier than you might suspect. Whereas in earlier times a good counterfeit required craftsmen skilled in photographic and fine printing techniques, in the current computer age a scanner, together with good ink, high-quality paper, and a laser printer can produce very adequate copies. So common had counterfeiting become, particularly in overseas countries desirous of dollars, that there were estimates that $2 billion in counterfeit money would be in circulation by the year 2000.

In the 1990s the U.S. Treasury Department began taking steps to safeguard American currency. Beginning with the $100 bill—the denomination most often counterfeited—they both altered the appearance of the bill and added several elements to make counterfeiting it more difficult. The most <u>conspicuous</u> change was the new portrait: not only was Ben Franklin's image changed and made larger, it was set off-center on the bill and printed with ink that would blur if photocopied. A watermark was also added. This image, which can be seen when a bill is held up to the light, is stamped into the currency paper as it is made and cannot be reproduced by scanner or copier. Security threads, also built into the paper, were a final safeguard. Filaments of yarn a few thousandths of an inch wide, these threads have identifying figures printed on them. A different filament is put into each denomination of money and set in a slightly different location.

Will these improvements, also made on other bills, stop counterfeiting altogether? Most likely not. But they will make it easier for anyone checking to identify and root out counterfeits.

Main Idea   1

	Answer	Score
Mark the *main idea*	M	15
Mark the statement that is *too broad*	B	5
Mark the statement that is *too narrow*	N	5

a. Because counterfeiting was so common, steps were taken to make it more difficult. ☐ _____

b. The $100 bill was the bill most often counterfeited. ☐ _____

c. With effort and skill, any currency can be counterfeited. ☐ _____

Subject Matter   **2**   Another title for this passage might be
- ☐ a. Protecting American Currency.
- ☐ b. The Desirable $100 Bill.
- ☐ c. Scanners and Watermarks.
- ☐ d. Playing Tricks on the U.S. Treasury.   _____

Supporting Details   **3**   Security threads
- ☐ a. are visible on the surface of each new bill.
- ☐ b. have identifying numbers on them.
- ☐ c. are made of colored silk.
- ☐ d. were replaced in the new bills by watermarks.   _____

Conclusion   **4**   The U.S. Treasury must have decided that
- ☐ a. only large bills were likely to be counterfeited.
- ☐ b. they could get rid of counterfeiters once and for all.
- ☐ c. a number of safeguards were needed to prevent counterfeiting.
- ☐ d. counterfeiters were usually trained in engraving.   _____

Clarifying Devices   **5**   Paragraph two is developed mostly through
- ☐ a. telling an anecdote.
- ☐ b. giving specific examples.
- ☐ c. comparing and contrasting.
- ☐ d. explaining the steps in a process.   _____

Vocabulary in Context   **6**   <u>Conspicuous</u> means
- ☐ a. very noticeable.
- ☐ b. quite dark.
- ☐ c. fearful.
- ☐ d. attractive.   _____

Add your scores for questions 1–6. Enter the total here and on the graph on page 218.   **Total Score**   _____

64 A Bitter Feud

They had lived deep in the Appalachian Mountains, on either side of the Tug Fork River, since well before the Civil War. They were backwoods people—hardworking, intelligent, and fiercely independent—and at various periods got along well enough to intermarry. But the Hatfields of West Virginia and the McCoys of Kentucky are remembered today for their involvement in a vicious family feud that lasted some 30 years and claimed at least 13 lives.

Hostilities grew between the families during the Civil War, when Harmon McCoy was murdered by the Hatfields for having served in the Union army. Several years later a claim that a Hatfield had stolen a McCoy pig led to a trial, an acquittal, and the subsequent murder by the McCoys of the witness who had gotten the accused Hatfield off. But it was a romance between two young members of the clans that <u>precipitated</u> the bloodiest era of the feud.

Roseanna McCoy ran off with Johnse Hatfield in 1880 to his family's home, where she was welcomed less than enthusiastically. Nor was her own family over-joyed when she returned a few months later—but they did swear revenge on Johnse. On the night they captured him, with murder their intent, Roseanna made a fateful decision to alert his kinfolk. Johnse escaped, but three of Roseanna's brothers eventually got even, attacking and killing an uncle of Johnse's at a public gathering. The three soon paid with their own lives, and a 10-year round of warfare began.

As for Roseanna, she ended up alone, renounced by both Hatfields and McCoys. Her death from sickness and depression before she was 30 made her one more victim of the feud.

Main Idea	1			
			Answer	Score
	Mark the *main idea*		M	15
	Mark the statement that is *too broad*		B	5
	Mark the statement that is *too narrow*		N	5

a. Family feuds can build from bad feelings all the way to murder. ☐ _____

b. The Hatfields and the McCoys lived near the Tug Fork River. ☐ _____

c. Over the years, hard feelings between Hatfields and McCoys led to violence and killings. ☐ _____

Score 15 points for each correct answer.   **Score**

Subject Matter   **2**   This passage focuses mainly on
☐ a. describing the life of backwoods people.
☐ b. explaining why there should be laws against family feuds.
☐ c. a trial involving a stolen pig.
☐ d. a history of the Hatfield-McCoy feud.   _____

Supporting Details   **3**   During the Civil War,
☐ a. the Hatfields and McCoys were at peace.
☐ b. hostilities between the families got worse.
☐ c. Roseanna ran away with Johnse.
☐ d. the Hatfields moved into the Tug Fork River area.   _____

Conclusion   **4**   Roseanna McCoy's family renounced her because
☐ a. she had stated that the Hatfields were kinder to her.
☐ b. she had warned Johnse that they were after him.
☐ c. her brothers had killed one of Johnse's uncles.
☐ d. she wanted to move out of the area entirely.   _____

Clarifying Devices   **5**   Another way to say "less than enthusiastically" would be
☐ a. "enthusiastically."
☐ b. "quietly."
☐ c. "happily."
☐ d. "grudgingly."   _____

Vocabulary in Context   **6**   In this passage <u>precipitated</u> means
☐ a. quickened the development of.
☐ b. delayed.
☐ c. demanded.
☐ d. insulted the participants of.   _____

Add your scores for questions 1–6. Enter the total here and on the graph on page 218.   **Total Score**   _____

65 Champlain's Choice of Friends

Samuel de Champlain was one of the greatest French explorers of the New World. Early in his pioneering Champlain made a choice of <u>allies</u> that was to have a tremendous influence on the course of history in North America.

Soon after landing on the North American coast, Champlain became friends with the Algonquin Indians. He and his men carried on their explorations of the wilderness in safety, accompanied by an Algonquin war party. Together they traveled hundreds of miles in large canoes, throughout Canada and the northern United States. While exploring the area surrounding what was eventually called Lake Champlain, they were confronted by members of the Iroquois tribe, rivals of the Algonquin. The Iroquois had never seen white people. When they spotted Champlain coming forward with their enemies, they halted in astonishment. When Champlain and his men opened fire upon them, the Iroquois quickly retreated, causing the Algonquin warriors to rejoice.

Although he didn't realize it, Champlain had started a bitter and bloody war that would last a hundred years. The Iroquois, a fierce and powerful people, never forgave the French for aiding the Algonquin. The Iroquois remained the most bitter enemies of France in the New World and later gladly helped the English drive the French from the Canadian shores.

Main Idea	1	Answer	Score
	Mark the *main idea*	M	15
	Mark the statement that is *too broad*	B	5
	Mark the statement that is *too narrow*	N	5

a. Without realizing what he was doing, Champlain made the Iroquois enemies of the French. ☐ _____

b. Samuel de Champlain was a great explorer. ☐ _____

c. Champlain befriended the Algonquin tribe. ☐ _____

Score 15 points for each correct answer.   Score

Subject Matter 2 The best alternate title for this passage would be
☐ a. The Fierce Iroquois.
☐ b. Indian Tribes of North America.
☐ c. Champlain and the Indians.
☐ d. Champlain's Explorations.   _____

**Supporting
Details** 3 The Algonquin
☐ a. were friends of the Iroquois.
☐ b. named Lake Champlain.
☐ c. were friends of the English.
☐ d. traveled with Champlain.   _____

Conclusion 4 This passage suggests that
☐ a. the Algonquin and the Iroquois had never
        been enemies before.
☐ b. Champlain wasn't very good at choosing his
        friends.
☐ c. choices may have unforeseen results.
☐ d. the Algonquin let the French down.   _____

**Clarifying
Devices** 5 The method in which the passage is presented
is primarily through
☐ a. argument.
☐ b. analogy.
☐ c. narrative.
☐ d. questioning.   _____

**Vocabulary
in Context** 6 The best definition for the word <u>allies</u> is
☐ a. enemies.
☐ b. guides.
☐ c. warriors.
☐ d. friends.   _____

**Add your scores for questions 1–6. Enter the total here   Total
and on the graph on page 218.   Score**   _____

66 An Ancient Puzzle

Perhaps you are an individual who enjoys working puzzles requiring that you trace your way through a network of confusing, conflicting, sometimes dead-end paths. If so, you have been seduced by a device that predates even the ancient Greeks: the maze.

Large, walk-through mazes, or labyrinths, have historically been regarded as sacred areas or gateways having magical powers; hence they frequently were positioned at the entrances of important ancient sites. One of the first recorded mentions of a maze is found in the myth of the Minotaur, a half-man, half-bull monster who devoured the flesh of the king's enemies until the hero Theseus threaded his way through the complex maze where the beast was imprisoned and slayed it. Despite this legend, ancient mazes generally consisted of only a single twisting path, with no intersections, and were often used for processions or <u>tranquil</u> walking and meditation.

Magical or religious significance continued to be associated with mazes built in the Middle Ages. Along the shore in Scandinavia stand numerous stone mazes that fishermen once walked through for luck as they went to sea. Mazes also grace the floors of many medieval cathedrals; by finding their way to the center, repentant sinners were believed to find their way back to God.

Eventually mazes came to be constructed mainly for pleasure. Royalty built elaborate mazes in their gardens from hedges, and public parks for the middle classes copied the structures.

Mazes are still constructed and enjoyed today. The cornfield maze built by a Wisconsin family—in the shape of their state—to celebrate 150 years of statehood is one striking example.

Main Idea	1	Answer	Score
	Mark the *main idea*	M	15
	Mark the statement that is *too broad*	B	5
	Mark the statement that is *too narrow*	N	5

a. Many mazes had religious significance connected to them. ☐ ____

b. Mazes have intrigued people from earliest times up to the present. ☐ ____

c. Many people enjoy mazes and other puzzles. ☐ ____

Subject Matter   **2**   Another appropriate title for this passage would be
- ☐ a. Gardens and Cornfields.
- ☐ b. The Magical Maze.
- ☐ c. Catching the Minotaur.
- ☐ d. Mazes Through the Ages.   _____

Supporting Details   **3**   Theseus
- ☐ a. found the Minotaur in the maze and killed it.
- ☐ b. joined the Minotaur in eating victims' flesh.
- ☐ c. built a maze for the Minotaur.
- ☐ d. never escaped from the Minotaur's maze.   _____

Conclusion   **4**   The Minotaur's maze must have been
- ☐ a. a place for religious worship.
- ☐ b. a single, twisting path with no intersections.
- ☐ c. a network of confusing, sometimes dead-end paths.
- ☐ d. built in Scandinavia.   _____

Clarifying Devices   **5**   The information in the passage is presented primarily
- ☐ a. in time order.
- ☐ b. as steps in a process.
- ☐ c. through descriptions of things one can hear.
- ☐ d. as an argument supporting the building of mazes.   _____

Vocabulary in Context   **6**   <u>Tranquil</u> means
- ☐ a. noisy.
- ☐ b. dangerous.
- ☐ c. confusing.
- ☐ d. quiet.   _____

Add your scores for questions 1–6. Enter the total here and on the graph on page 218.   **Total Score**   _____

67 A Dinosaur Named Sue

Just what is the value of a dinosaur fossil? If it is one of the most complete Tyrannosaurus Rex skeletons ever discovered, the price can be in the millions. And whose is it to buy and sell? This is a complicated question: consider the case of, and the controversy over, the T. rex named Sue.

Sue—named for its discoverer, Susan Hendrickson—was unearthed on a South Dakota ranch in 1990. The head of the discovery team, Peter Larson from the Black Hills Institute of Geological Research, presented ranch owner Maurice Williams with a check for $5,000 and carted the skeleton away. Almost immediately, however, controversy erupted as to whether a legal sale had ensued. Williams, a Native American, states he told Larson at the time that the fossil, since it had been discovered on land held in <u>trust</u> by the government, could not be sold without the government's approval. And Larson certainly must have realized that $5,000 was an incredibly cheap price for a fossil that was 90 percent complete.

Following several years of bitter legal wrangles, Williams ultimately earned the right to the skeleton (Larson earned himself a felony conviction). But then a second battle of sorts began, a legal and scientific debate over whether such an exceedingly rare fossil should become the property of a museum, where the public would have access to it, or be sold to a private collector.

In 1997 Sue was finally sold at auction. In slightly over an hour, the original $500,000 asking price quickly escalated to $7.6 million, and Sue was bought by Chicago's Field Museum, which vowed to have the fossil on display within two years. As for Maurice Williams, he received the bulk of the proceeds—tax-free because of his trust arrangement with the government.

Main Idea   1

	Answer	Score
Mark the *main idea*	M	15
Mark the statement that is *too broad*	B	5
Mark the statement that is *too narrow*	N	5

a. Sue was discovered on a South Dakota ranch. ☐ _____

b. Some dinosaur skeletons are extremely valuable. ☐ _____

c. Both the ownership and the sale of Sue were sources of controversy. ☐ _____

Subject Matter **2** This passage is mostly about
- ☐ a. the discovery of Sue.
- ☐ b. installing Sue in a museum.
- ☐ c. battles over Sue.
- ☐ d. why Sue is so valuable.   _____

Supporting Details **3** Sue was named after
- ☐ a. the dinosaur's legal owner.
- ☐ b. the dinosaur expert at the Field Museum.
- ☐ c. the woman who discovered it.
- ☐ d. the woman on whose ranch it was found.   _____

Conclusion **4** This passage suggests that
- ☐ a. Larson tried to take advantage of Williams.
- ☐ b. treasures like Sue are safer in the hands of private investors.
- ☐ c. Susan Hendrickson should have kept the dinosaur.
- ☐ d. 90-percent-complete dinosaur fossils are fairly common.   _____

Clarifying Devices **5** The author builds reader interest in the first paragraph by
- ☐ a. asking questions.
- ☐ b. explaining where the name Sue came from.
- ☐ c. telling exactly how much Sue sold for.
- ☐ d. summarizing how the dinosaur was found.   _____

Vocabulary in Context **6** In this passage <u>trust</u> means
- ☐ a. belief.
- ☐ b. safe-keeping.
- ☐ c. confidence.
- ☐ d. a bank.   _____

Add your scores for questions 1–6. Enter the total here and on the graph on page 218.   **Total Score**   _____

68 The Best Movie of All

Assemble a group of film critics, famous or otherwise, and ask them to identify the greatest movie of all time. The vast majority will select Orson Welles's 1941 master work *Citizen Kane*.

What is it that makes this movie so great? Not necessarily just the subject matter—an account of the rise and fall of business tycoon Charles Foster Kane that was inspired in many ways by the life of publishing magnate William Randolph Hearst. The film is impressive because of *how* the story is told and the camera and film techniques that are used to heighten the drama.

As the film opens, the dying Kane mutters the single word "Rosebud," a mysterious utterance that induces a curious reporter to unravel its meaning. By interviewing Kane's closest associates, all of whom convey their versions of his life in flashback form, the reporter/narrator ultimately pieces together an unforgettable portrait of Kane's rapid rise and tragic decline.

Flashbacks had been used in earlier films, but never in such an out-of-sequence style, and never strung together with newsreel footage that clarified the focus of each. Equally novel were many of the camera shots—the shadows they created, the background objects they highlighted. One famous scene shows multiple images of Kane reflected through parallel mirrors. Another, shot from floor level, highlights a character's staggering drunkenness. Welles even planned the exact distance between characters in most scenes, always seeking the strongest effect. It is the combination of these techniques, along with a compelling story, that makes *Citizen Kane* great.

And what is the significance of "Rosebud"? See the movie to find out.

Main Idea 1

	Answer	Score
Mark the *main idea*	M	15
Mark the statement that is *too broad*	B	5
Mark the statement that is *too narrow*	N	5

a. As he dies, Kane whispers the word "Rosebud." ☐ _____

b. According to many film critics, *Citizen Kane* is the greatest movie of all time. ☐ _____

c. There were many great movies made in the 1940s. ☐ _____

Subject Matter   **2**   This passage deals primarily with

☐ a. a history of movies in the 1940s.

☐ b. the things that made *Citizen Kane* great.

☐ c. the various movies that Orson Welles made.

☐ d. the significance of "Rosebud."   _____

Supporting Details   **3**   The story of Kane is based on the life of

☐ a. Orson Welles.

☐ b. William Randolph Hearst.

☐ c. a hard-working reporter.

☐ d. a well-known movie critic of the 1940s.   _____

Conclusion   **4**   The newsreel footage in *Citizen Kane* was used to

☐ a. tie together various people's stories about Kane.

☐ b. show that Kane was involved in newspaper publishing.

☐ c. emphasize clever camera shots.

☐ d. give background information about Orson Welles.   _____

Clarifying Devices   **5**   The passage gives examples of

☐ a. newspaper headlines in the movie.

☐ b. great camera shots in the movie.

☐ c. details about Kane that are revealed in flashbacks.

☐ d. reviewers' comments about the movie.   _____

Vocabulary in Context   **6**   <u>Convey</u> in this passage means

☐ a. send.

☐ b. make known.

☐ c. lie about.

☐ d. pretend to understand.   _____

Add your scores for questions 1–6. Enter the total here and on the graph on page 218.   **Total Score**   _____

69 Beyond the Call of Duty

The marathon, a regular event in the Olympic games, received its name from the Greek plain of Marathon, where a battle between the Persian army, led by King Darius, and the Athenian army was fought in 490 B.C.

Darius's troops had arrived on Marathon and were preparing to attack Athens. The Athenians were greatly outnumbered by the Persians, so they sent a runner, Pheidippides, to Sparta to request aid against the attackers. Pheidippides ran the 140 miles to Sparta in about 24 hours. After receiving a promise of help from the Spartans, he ran back to deliver the news to his countrymen, again covering the rocky <u>terrain</u> in 24 hours.

Pheidippides fought in the battle of Marathon several days later. The Spartans didn't come to their aid in time, but the Athenians were victorious anyway; so the commander of the army wanted to notify the citizens of Athens of the Persians' defeat. The battle-weary Pheidippides, who had had little time to recover from his 280-mile run of the previous week, agreed once again to be the messenger.

Pheidippides set off on the nearly 25-mile-long trek from Marathon to Athens, running into the Athenian marketplace just a few hours later. He managed to gasp "Rejoice, we conquer," then dropped dead in his tracks before the astounded onlookers.

The marathon footrace was established as an Olympic event in honor of Pheidippides. The official distance for a marathon is 26 miles, 385 yards.

Main Idea 1

	Answer	Score
Mark the *main idea*	M	15
Mark the statement that is *too broad*	B	5
Mark the statement that is *too narrow*	N	5

a. Pheidippides was a Greek hero in whose honor the marathon footrace was instituted. ☐ ____

b. Pheidippides is a hero of Greek history. ☐ ____

c. Pheidippides ran as a messenger for the Athenian army. ☐ ____

Subject Matter   **2**   This passage deals mainly with
- ☐ a. a battle between the Greeks and the Romans.
- ☐ b. the origin of the Olympic event called the marathon.
- ☐ c. a Greek runner's heroic endurance.
- ☐ d. the Athenian army's victory against the Persian army.

_____

Supporting Details   **3**   Pheidippides first ran to
- ☐ a. request supplies from neighbors.
- ☐ b. announce that the Persians were going to attack Sparta.
- ☐ c. request aid from allies.
- ☐ d. demand reasons for the attack.

_____

Conclusion   **4**   We can conclude from this passage that
- ☐ a. Pheidippides loved his country.
- ☐ b. the Athenian commander was merciless.
- ☐ c. the Spartans didn't want to help the Athenians.
- ☐ d. marathon races are difficult to run.

_____

Clarifying Devices   **5**   The words "battle-weary Pheidippides" are meant to make the reader feel
- ☐ a. angry toward the Persians.
- ☐ b. interested in the battle.
- ☐ c. bored with the outcome of the battle.
- ☐ d. sympathetic toward Pheidippides.

_____

Vocabulary in Context   **6**   <u>Terrain</u> means
- ☐ a. hills.
- ☐ b. paths.
- ☐ c. plain.
- ☐ d. land.

_____

Add your scores for questions 1–6. Enter the total here and on the graph on page 218.   **Total Score** _____

70 Living Twice

In 1952 an American housewife named Virginia Tighe was hypnotized and began to talk about her previous life as an Irish girl named Bridey Murphy. In 1956 a book called *The Search for Bridey Murphy* was written about her experience, and it became a best-seller. Thousands of people believed that it gave solid evidence for reincarnation—the rebirth of the soul into another body. They flocked to hypnotists to find out what their <u>former</u> lives had been like.

Of course, not everyone immediately believed that Virginia Tighe had lived a previous life in Ireland. It was impressive that she spoke with an Irish accent when under hypnosis, but some people looked for further proof. They went all the way to Ireland to find the places she mentioned and to look for records of a girl named Bridey Murphy. They didn't find anything definite, but some people closer to home did—in Virginia's hometown of Chicago, Illinois. In Chicago they found a woman whose maiden name had been Bridey Murphy and who had lived across the street from Virginia. They found people who remembered that in high school Virginia had liked to talk with an Irish accent. When Virginia was a child, relatives had told her stories about things that had happened to them, and these stories were just like those remembered by Bridey Murphy. In short, there was no evidence at all that Virginia remembered anything from a previous life—only things from her own childhood. Bridey Murphy was just a fantasy, popular with people who wanted a reason to believe in reincarnation.

Main Idea 1		
	Answer	Score
Mark the *main idea*	M	15
Mark the statement that is *too broad*	B	5
Mark the statement that is *too narrow*	N	5

a. Virginia Tighe claimed to have lived a previous life as an Irish girl named Bridey Murphy. ☐ _____

b. Many people believe in reincarnation. ☐ _____

c. People who went to Ireland found no records of Bridey Murphy. ☐ _____

Score 15 points for each correct answer.

Score

Subject Matter   **2**   This passage focuses on
- ☐ a. the use of hypnotism.
- ☐ b. Irish immigrants.
- ☐ c. Virginia Tighe's story.
- ☐ d. a best-selling book.

_____

Supporting Details   **3**   What is mentioned as one reason that people believed Virginia Tighe once lived in Ireland?
- ☐ a. Her relatives told stories about it.
- ☐ b. Her hair was red.
- ☐ c. Records were found in Chicago.
- ☐ d. She had an Irish accent when hypnotized.

_____

Conclusion   **4**   The author suggests that the book _The Search for Bridey Murphy_ became a best-seller because
- ☐ a. it was a very well-written, exciting story.
- ☐ b. several churches recommended it as a true story.
- ☐ c. Bridey Murphy was a famous Irish saint.
- ☐ d. many people wanted to believe in reincarnation.

_____

Clarifying Devices   **5**   To support the view that the Bridey Murphy reincarnation was a fantasy, the author uses
- ☐ a. humor and sarcasm.
- ☐ b. several facts.
- ☐ c. an emotional appeal.
- ☐ d. logical argument.

_____

Vocabulary in Context   **6**   Which word could best be substituted for <u>former</u>?
- ☐ a. previous
- ☐ b. primitive
- ☐ c. usual
- ☐ d. first

_____

Add your scores for questions 1–6. Enter the total here and on the graph on page 218.

Total Score _____

71 Queen of the Nile

Legend has made Cleopatra one of the world's best-known women and has created an image of her that is both incomplete and greatly <u>embellished</u>. Thanks to Shakespeare and other writers, she is thought of as a dark Egyptian seductress and pursuer of powerful men, a woman who was ruled by passion to such an extent that she killed herself over the death of her lover Mark Antony. The truth? Well, to begin with, Cleopatra was blond, not dark, and, despite the fact that she ruled Egypt, she was actually Greek.

Examination of the historical record doesn't support the notion that Cleopatra pursued men to any great extent. In fact, there is no evidence connecting her to any men other than first Julius Caesar and then Mark Antony. Her relationship with Antony did not begin until four years after Caesar's death. Both unions were recognized in Egypt as marriages, and she was apparently a faithful and helpful wife to both men.

Much has been made of the Queen of the Nile's beauty, yet one contemporary observer wrote that her looks were far from remarkable. Her passionate nature has also been overemphasized. But her impressive knowledge of languages and skill in military strategy and political negotiations have been either ignored or forgotten.

Then there is the belief that Cleopatra killed herself for love. The truth is that she coolly ended her life in order to avoid humiliation and execution at the hands of Egypt's conqueror, Augustus Caesar.

Main Idea	1		
		Answer	Score
	Mark the *main idea*	M	15
	Mark the statement that is *too broad*	B	5
	Mark the statement that is *too narrow*	N	5

a. There are a great many misconceptions about the legendary Cleopatra. ☐ _____

b. Cleopatra knew many languages and was skilled in military and political strategy. ☐ _____

c. Legend often distorts the images of historical figures. ☐ _____

Subject Matter   **2**   The best alternative title for this passage would be

☐ a. The Beauty of Cleopatra.

☐ b. Cleopatra's Roman Marriages.

☐ c. The Truth About the Queen of the Nile.

☐ d. A Legendary Woman.

_____

Supporting Details   **3**   According to the passage, it is not true that Cleopatra was

☐ a. married twice.

☐ b. an Egyptian.

☐ c. politically skillful.

☐ d. a Greek.

_____

Conclusion   **4**   We can infer that Cleopatra

☐ a. didn't really rule Egypt, because she was Greek.

☐ b. allowed Caesar and Antony to rule for her.

☐ c. was an incompetent ruler.

☐ d. took an active role in political and military affairs.

_____

Clarifying Devices   **5**   In the second paragraph, "first" and "then" are used to indicate

☐ a. an important spatial relationship.

☐ b. emphasis on particular points.

☐ c. the order of events.

☐ d. the relative importance of two items.

_____

Vocabulary in Context   **6**   In this context, <u>embellished</u> means

☐ a. having few strong characteristics.

☐ b. filled with interesting but untrue details.

☐ c. filled with deliberate lies.

☐ d. changed according to the whims of historians.

_____

Add your scores for questions 1–6. Enter the total here and on the graph on page 218.   **Total Score**

_____

72 The World's Largest Diamond

In 1907 King Edward VII of England received an <u>extravagant</u> present for his 66th birthday: a diamond that weighed 3,106 carats.

This raw, rough diamond was found on January 25, 1905, in South Africa, where a mine superintendent named Frederick Wells stumbled across it while inspecting the Premier Mine before closing it down for the day. The diamond, named after Thomas Cullinan, the founder of the mine, turned out to be the largest diamond ever discovered. Wells not only picked up a gigantic precious stone that day, he also garnered for himself a $10,000 reward.

South Africa still being part of the British Commonwealth at that time, the government purchased the huge uncut stone as a fitting gift for its monarch. When King Edward finally received his priceless present it was still in its original form, so he had to have the diamond properly cut and polished. After a lengthy search, Joseph Asscher, a Dutch craftsman, was chosen to perform the delicate operation.

In 1908 after weeks of study and inspection, Joseph Asscher finally concluded that the best plan was to cleave the Cullinan diamond into nine major stones, 96 lesser gems, and 10 carats of polished fragments.

The most magnificent of the nine major stones cut from the Cullinan is the 530-carat, pear-shaped gem known as the Great Star of Africa. Today this stone is part of the royal scepter of the British crown jewels, which are carefully guarded in the Tower of London.

Main Idea	1		
		Answer	**Score**
Mark the *main idea*		M	15
Mark the statement that is *too broad*		B	5
Mark the statement that is *too narrow*		N	5

a. Diamonds are magnificent gems worthy of a king. ☐ _____

b. The Cullinan diamond is part of the crown jewels of England. ☐ _____

c. The Cullinan diamond was the largest and most magnificent diamond ever found. ☐ _____

Subject Matter   **2**   What is the main subject of the passage?

☐ a. King Edward VII

☐ b. Joseph Asscher

☐ c. the British crown jewels

☐ d. the Cullinan diamond   _____

Supporting Details   **3**   The Cullinan diamond was found in the

☐ a. South African Mine.

☐ b. Premier Mine.

☐ c. Nile Mine.

☐ d. Wells Mine.   _____

Conclusion   **4**   You can assume from this passage that

☐ a. King Edward VII was fond of diamonds.

☐ b. the Cullinan diamond was hard to find.

☐ c. Frederick Wells liked King Edward VII.

☐ d. Joseph Asscher was skilled at cutting diamonds.   _____

Clarifying Devices   **5**   In the first sentence, the writer calls attention to the subject by telling about an incredible

☐ a. piece of rock.

☐ b. birthday gift.

☐ c. sparkler.

☐ d. crown jewel.   _____

Vocabulary in Context   **6**   In this passage extravagant means

☐ a. rare.

☐ b. very impractical.

☐ c. extremely nice.

☐ d. tasteful.   _____

Add your scores for questions 1–6. Enter the total here and on the graph on page 218.   **Total Score**   _____

73 A Short History of Sitcoms

Sitcoms—or situation comedies—have been around since the beginning days of television. Frequently involving families, these early programs conveyed an image of American domestic life that became the yardstick against which many 1950s families measured themselves.

Premiering in 1951, "I Love Lucy" was not only one of the earliest family sitcoms, it also in many ways changed the face of television. This show was the first to be filmed and recorded before a live studio audience, thus providing a laugh track. It was also the first program to use three separate cameras, thereby allowing a much greater diversity of shots. And finally, it introduced a ditzy but clever female lead character whose personality would be copied in many other sitcoms.

"I Love Lucy" notwithstanding, other sitcoms presented more "typical" TV families. These generally included a wise father, always dressed in suit and tie, whose job was either unknown or nonexistent; a warm, supportive mother who always deferred to the father; and two or three children whose minor scrapes were always resolved by program's end. "The Donna Reed Show," "Father Knows Best," and "Leave It to Beaver" were popular shows in this mold.

The antecedent of the family sitcom as we know it today was in many ways "All in the Family." This program replaced the lovable but idealized sitcom dad with a bigoted, ill-tempered loudmouth who seemed like someone we actually knew. "All in the Family" ushered in the era of more preposterous but ultimately more realistic sitcoms that still are popular today.

Main Idea 1

	Answer	Score
Mark the *main idea*	M	15
Mark the statement that is *too broad*	B	5
Mark the statement that is *too narrow*	N	5

a. "The Donna Reed Show" and "Leave It to Beaver" were typical family sitcoms. ☐ _____

b. Early sitcoms show an idealistic picture of American life that later became more realistic. ☐ _____

c. Sitcoms on TV have always been popular. ☐ _____

Subject Matter   2   This passage is mainly about
- ☐ a. how "I Love Lucy" changed television.
- ☐ b. early television programs.
- ☐ c. the picture of American life that sitcoms have painted.
- ☐ d. wise fathers and supportive mothers.   _____

Supporting Details   3   One big change in "All in the Family" was that
- ☐ a. the father was unpleasant but more realistic.
- ☐ b. there was no mother in the family.
- ☐ c. it had children who idolized their father.
- ☐ d. it was filmed with three cameras.   _____

Conclusion   4   This passage suggests that
- ☐ a. families in the 1950s were nicer to each other than modern families.
- ☐ b. "I Love Lucy" used many new techniques, but it was not popular.
- ☐ c. real families in the 1950s wanted to be like TV sitcom families.
- ☐ d. "All in the Family" was not a change for the better in TV programming.   _____

Clarifying Devices   5   The author mentions shows like "Father Knows Best" and "Leave It to Beaver"
- ☐ a. as examples of "typical" TV families.
- ☐ b. to point out their similarities with "I Love Lucy."
- ☐ c. to praise the way they portrayed families.
- ☐ d. to argue that TV today should return to those kinds of shows.   _____

Vocabulary in Context   6   In this passage <u>deferred</u> means
- ☐ a. delayed.
- ☐ b. gave in to.
- ☐ c. argued with.
- ☐ d. ignored.   _____

Add your scores for questions 1–6. Enter the total here and on the graph on page 218.   **Total Score**   _____

74 The Deadly Nuisance

D. H. Lawrence assailed it as "that small, high, hateful bugle." The creature he was speaking of was the mosquito. Most of us think of her—only the females bite—as merely a summertime nuisance. We barricade ourselves behind screens, invest in insect repellent, and finally apply lotions when we inevitably get bitten. But for centuries the mosquito has been recognized as more than an inconvenience. It is also a carrier of some of the world's deadliest diseases.

As a disease transmitter, the mosquito has been most frequently associated with the fever and chills of malaria. Although the United States and most developed nations have now either eradicated or significantly controlled this disease, malaria still afflicts more than 150 million people in the tropics, killing more than a million children a year in Africa alone.

Yellow fever is another disease carried by mosquitoes. It has been brought under control in North America, so we tend to think of it as an exotic disease. But though it is now confined to Africa and South America, it retains its deadly power.

Encephalitis, which can cause brain damage or death, is one mosquito-borne human disease that still appears in the United States. Common birds carry this disease too, but it's the pesky mosquito that transmits it to people. Most of the time, your risk of contracting encephalitis is <u>minimal</u>, but the chances increase when the mosquito population swells. So remember, screens and insect repellent may be protection from much more than a mere nuisance.

Main Idea	1		
		Answer	Score
	Mark the *main idea*	**M**	15
	Mark the statement that is *too broad*	**B**	5
	Mark the statement that is *too narrow*	**N**	5
	a. Mosquitoes are carriers of deadly disease, in addition to being pests.	☐	_____
	b. People tend to think of the mosquito as a simple nuisance.	☐	_____
	c. Many animals and insects transmit disease to humans.	☐	_____

Subject Matter **2** This passage is primarily about
- [ ] a. the causes of malaria and yellow fever.
- [ ] b. how mosquitoes bite their victims.
- [ ] c. diseases carried by insects.
- [ ] d. the mosquito's function as a disease carrier.   _____

Supporting Details **3** According to the passage, people in the U.S. still have a chance of contracting
- [ ] a. yellow fever.
- [ ] b. encephalitis.
- [ ] c. malaria.
- [ ] d. filariasis.   _____

Conclusion **4** The final sentence of the passage implies that the writer thinks
- [ ] a. disease-carrying mosquitoes still pose a significant threat.
- [ ] b. screens and insect repellent are ineffective protection against mosquitoes.
- [ ] c. the threat of disease being transmitted by mosquitoes no longer exists in the U.S.
- [ ] d. screens and insect repellent are the best protection against mosquitoes.   _____

Clarifying Devices **5** The writer quotes D. H. Lawrence's description of the mosquito to
- [ ] a. help the reader visualize the insect's appearance.
- [ ] b. convey factual information.
- [ ] c. catch the reader's attention.
- [ ] d. contrast it with his own description.   _____

Vocabulary in Context **6** The word <u>minimal</u> is closest in meaning to
- [ ] a. nonexistent.
- [ ] b. frightening.
- [ ] c. average.
- [ ] d. slight.   _____

Add your scores for questions 1–6. Enter the total here and on the graph on page 218.   **Total Score**   _____

75 Putting the Pieces Together

A simple form of this amusement may be one of the earliest challenges faced by a toddler as he or she begins developing spatial awareness. Older children may use variations of it, by themselves or with adults, either for pleasure or as a relatively painless way to learn geography. And adults may spend weeks struggling to assemble a 500-, 1000-, or 1500-piece version of it.

The item in question is, of course, the jigsaw puzzle. Some researchers find early puzzle prototypes in ancient Greece and Egypt, but there is fairly general agreement that the direct ancestor of today's puzzles was created by John Spilsbury in the 1760s. Spilsbury, a London print-shop owner and mapmaker, mounted one of his maps on a thin mahogany board and cut out each country with a hand-held fret saw. The immediate success of his product as a learning tool for children created a booming market for all sorts of educational puzzles. Alphabets, charts and tables, and historical scenes were a few of the subjects of these finely made, expensive works.

The pieces of the early puzzles were usually not interlocking, except for the edge pieces: the task of cutting them by hand was too <u>arduous</u>. It was not until the introduction of the jigsaw in the 1870s that mass-produced puzzles with uniform-shaped pieces made their appearance.

Jigsaw puzzles for adults became generally available in the early 1900s. Still often made of plywood and still quite expensive, they quickly became a popular amusement. Records show that new ones were often purchased on Saturday mornings as the weekend's entertainment and that for a time they superseded cards as the most popular game at social gatherings.

Main Idea	1			Answer	Score
		Mark the *main idea*		M	15
		Mark the statement that is *too broad*		B	5
		Mark the statement that is *too narrow*		N	5
	a.	Early puzzles were made of wood.		☐	_____
	b.	Some educational devices are several hundred years old.		☐	_____
	c.	First developed as learning tools for children, puzzles soon became popular amusements for everyone.		☐	_____

Subject Matter   2   This passage is primarily about
- [ ] a. children in the 1700s.
- [ ] b. a search for new family amusements.
- [ ] c. jigsaw puzzles in ancient Greece and Egypt.
- [ ] d. how jigsaw puzzles came to be developed.   _____

Supporting Details   3   The first puzzles that John Spilsbury made showed
- [ ] a. famous paintings.
- [ ] b. charts and tables.
- [ ] c. letters of the alphabet.
- [ ] d. maps.   _____

Conclusion   4   The passage implies that puzzles became less expensive when
- [ ] a. the jigsaw was developed.
- [ ] b. adults began buying them.
- [ ] c. they were no longer made of wood.
- [ ] d. more children began going to public schools.   _____

Clarifying Devices   5   The writer builds interest in the first paragraph by
- [ ] a. asking a series of questions.
- [ ] b. giving clues to the topic, but not directly identifying it.
- [ ] c. giving the early history of puzzles.
- [ ] d. comparing puzzles to mazes.   _____

Vocabulary in Context   6   The word <u>arduous</u> means
- [ ] a. easy.
- [ ] b. boring.
- [ ] c. difficult.
- [ ] d. noisy.   _____

Add your scores for questions 1–6. Enter the total here and on the graph on page 218.   **Total Score**   _____

76 Life on a Coral Reef

Anyone who enjoys watching colorful fish in an aquarium would really get a thrill out of swimming around a coral reef. Coral reefs are the natural homes of many of the brightly colored tropical fish sold in pet stores. Reefs are formed in warm, shallow seas such as the waters off the northeast coast of Australia, where the world's longest coral reef is situated. Reefs such as this one provide homes for countless small sea plants, mollusks, and crustaceans that in turn feed a host of fishes.

A swimmer or diver among the coral will easily spot the striking black-and-yellow pattern of the black angelfish and the many bright colors—yellow, red, green, and blue—of parrot fish. Smaller fish such as blueheads, yellow grunts, and butterfly fish swarm around the fantastic shapes of the coral—and the <u>predatory</u> attackers that feed on them swim there, too. The viciously toothed head of a moray eel can be seen peering from a crack. The thin, torpedo-like shape coasting slowly above the reef signals the presence of that solitary hunter the barracuda. Entire schools of the predatory gray snapper patrol the borders of the reef, looking for fish, crabs, or shrimp to add to their diet. The colorful and graceful fish inhabiting the coral reef include a wide range of sizes and types, from the delicate beauty of the little seaweed grazers to the deadly, streamlined shapes of the killers.

Main Idea	1	Answer	Score
	Mark the *main idea*	M	15
	Mark the statement that is *too broad*	B	5
	Mark the statement that is *too narrow*	N	5

a. Coral reefs are the hunting grounds of moray eels and barracudas. ☐ _____

b. The oceans are filled with an enormous variety of sea plants and animals. ☐ _____

c. Coral reefs are the homes of many kinds of tropical fish. ☐ _____

Subject Matter   **2**   This passage deals with
- ☐ a. swimmers and scuba divers.
- ☐ b. coral reefs.
- ☐ c. fishes of the coral reefs.
- ☐ d. schools of fish.

_____

Supporting Details   **3**   Coral cannot be found in
- ☐ a. tropical waters.
- ☐ b. the Caribbean.
- ☐ c. the Arctic Ocean.
- ☐ d. shallow waters.

_____

Conclusion   **4**   The author admires
- ☐ a. the variety of colors in a coral reef.
- ☐ b. warm, shallow seas.
- ☐ c. the daring diver who seeks adventure.
- ☐ d. the size of the coral reefs.

_____

Clarifying Devices   **5**   The writer describes the beauty of life among the coral reefs by using
- ☐ a. comparisons.
- ☐ b. supporting statements.
- ☐ c. adjectives.
- ☐ d. contrasts.

_____

Vocabulary in Context   **6**   A <u>predatory</u> fish is one that
- ☐ a. is foolish.
- ☐ b. eats other creatures.
- ☐ c. swims fast.
- ☐ d. is protective.

_____

Add your scores for questions 1–6. Enter the total here and on the graph on page 218.   **Total Score**   _____

77 Understanding Ebola

Disaster movies often portray catastrophes that destroy, or at least threaten to destroy, Earth's entire population. In fact, a virus emerged in the 1970s that could have been just that <u>lethal</u>.

Named after a river that traverses the Congo, the Ebola virus originally manifested itself in the interior of Africa in 1976. Two strains of the disease, with almost identical symptoms, affected humans: Ebola Zaire and Ebola Sudan. The Sudan version was deadly enough, killing 50 percent of those it infected; however, Zaire, with its 90 percent mortality rate, was even worse.

The origins—though not the cause—of Ebola Sudan can be traced back to a single individual in a Sudanese town. Ebola Zaire seemed to erupt in over 50 villages simultaneously. Both strains quickly invaded local hospitals, where needle sharing and other unsanitary practices ensured the rapid spreading of the infection by bringing people into contact with contaminated blood. If the virus had been capable of spreading through the air, or if one infected person had unknowingly entered a large population center, Ebola might have become a worldwide epidemic.

However, soon after these fierce outbreaks the virus died out, at least temporarily. Ebola was so lethal and killed so quickly (in a matter of days) that within a short period of time there was no one around to infect. Hospital workers in at least one case deserted their workplace in panic, thus halting the administering of potentially unclean, disease-spreading injections.

But Ebola has not disappeared. With no known vaccination or cure in the offing, it seems only a matter of time until another epidemic erupts.

Main Idea	1		
		Answer	**Score**
	Mark the *main idea*	☒ M	15
	Mark the statement that is *too broad*	☒ B	5
	Mark the statement that is *too narrow*	☒ N	5

a. Many deadly diseases have no known cure. ☐ _____

b. The deadly Ebola virus strikes without warning and then dies out just as quickly. ☐ _____

c. Two strains of Ebola affect humans: Ebola Sudan and Ebola Zaire. ☐ _____

Score 15 points for each correct answer.   **Score**

Subject Matter   **2**   Another appropriate title for this passage is
☐ a. A Quick and Frightening Killer.
☐ b. How Ebola Zaire Differs from Ebola Sudan.
☐ c. Diseases of Africa.
☐ d. The Dangers of Needle Sharing.   _____

Supporting Details   **3**   Of people stricken with Ebola Zaire, what percent die?
☐ a. 10 percent
☐ b. 50 percent
☐ c. 80 percent
☐ d. 90 percent   _____

Conclusion   **4**   One of the easiest places for Ebola to spread is
☐ a. out in the countryside.
☐ b. near a river.
☐ c. in a hospital.
☐ d. in a factory.   _____

Clarifying Devices   **5**   In paragraphs 2 and 3, the author explains Ebola Zaire and Ebola Sudan by
☐ a. mentioning similarities between them.
☐ b. mentioning differences between them.
☐ c. telling why there is a possible cure for only one of them.
☐ d. comparing them to the type of Ebola that only affects monkeys.   _____

Vocabulary in Context   **6**   The word <u>lethal</u> means
☐ a. noticeable.
☐ b. frightening.
☐ c. deadly.
☐ d. unusual.   _____

Add your scores for questions 1–6. Enter the total here and on the graph on page 218.   **Total Score**   _____

78 The Greatly Feared Octopus

The octopus's reputation as a human-killer isn't simply an exaggeration—it's a total myth. The octopus can indeed be a deadly hunter, but it attacks only its natural prey. Clams, mussels, crabs, lobsters, and an occasional sick or unwary fish have reason to be frightened of this multi-armed predator, but a human being is much too large to interest even the largest octopus. Even a giant among octopuses is much smaller than most people imagine. Far from being large enough to <u>engulf</u> a submarine, as monster octopuses in movies have been known to do, the largest octopuses, which are found on the Pacific coast, weigh around 110 pounds and grow to a diameter of no more than 10 feet.

It is difficult to understand why so many people consider octopuses to be dangerous creatures. The hard, parrotlike beak of an octopus is not used for attacking deep-sea divers but for cutting open crabs and lobsters. Indeed, the octopus possesses such a tiny throat that it cannot even swallow large pieces of meat. It feeds instead by pouring digestive juices into its victims and then sucking up the soupy remains. A clam, oyster, or scallop that finds itself in the grasp of an octopus has only a short time to live. But human beings are perfectly safe around octopuses. Still, people rarely care to venture close enough to these timid underwater creatures to get a good look at them.

Main Idea	1	Answer	Score
	Mark the *main idea*	M	15
	Mark the statement that is *too broad*	B	5
	Mark the statement that is *too narrow*	N	5

a. The octopus is not dangerous as many people believe it to be. ☐ _____

b. People often fear creatures that are not dangerous to them. ☐ _____

c. The octopus only hunts its natural prey. ☐ _____

Subject Matter   **2**   This passage is mainly about
    ☐ a. the horrors of the octopus.
    ☐ b. the largest octopus in the world.
    ☐ c. octopuses' deadly hunting methods.
    ☐ d. octopuses and their behavior.   _____

Supporting Details   **3**   The passage states that octopuses
    ☐ a. use their eight tentacles to catch their prey.
    ☐ b. always catch sick and careless fish.
    ☐ c. never attack people.
    ☐ d. can engulf submarines.   _____

Conclusion   **4**   You would not expect octopuses to
    ☐ a. kill clams.
    ☐ b. approach divers underwater.
    ☐ c. hide from danger.
    ☐ d. suck up their prey.   _____

Clarifying Devices   **5**   The author attempts to dispel people's misplaced fears about octopuses by
    ☐ a. contrasting facts with common misconceptions.
    ☐ b. telling lies about the creatures.
    ☐ c. pretending to like octopuses.
    ☐ d. making jokes about ocean life.   _____

Vocabulary in Context   **6**   <u>Engulf</u> means
    ☐ a. surround.
    ☐ b. beach.
    ☐ c. kill.
    ☐ d. out race.   _____

Add your scores for questions 1–6. Enter the total here and on the graph on page 218.   **Total Score**   _____

79 Helping the Farm Worker

Reformers are men and women who see situations that they consider unfair and then set forth to <u>remedy</u> them. Sometimes these individuals enjoy quick victories; just as frequently, however, the gains are slow in coming and easy to lose. But lasting change is never achieved easily, and a true reformer is ultimately measured by the worthiness of the cause as well as by its success.

Cesar Chavez's cause was the struggle of the migrant farm worker. As a boy growing up in Arizona in the 1930s, Chavez saw his own father lose his farm and be forced into a transient worker's lifestyle. Chavez himself worked full time in the fields from eighth grade on.

After a stint in the Navy in World War II, Chavez returned to California to begin trying to organize poor transient workers, most of them of Mexican heritage, into a union where they could fight for fairer living and working conditions. The struggle was difficult, for the farm owners were clever and the laborers easily intimidated. But in 1962 the National Farm Workers Association was established, and the group enjoyed early success and political support. A 1965 strike against California grape growers elicited the backing of Robert F. Kennedy and resulted in the first-ever contracts for migrant workers in the United States. A successful boycott of lettuce followed.

Unfortunately, a long downhill slide then began. By the time of Chavez's death in 1993, migrant workers had lost many of the advantages Chavez had gained for them. Chavez's supporters, however, believing his cause to be just, remain confident that conditions will once again improve for workers and that the reforms that Chavez fought for will be reinstituted.

Main Idea	1		
		Answer	**Score**
	Mark the *main idea*	M	15
	Mark the statement that is *too broad*	B	5
	Mark the statement that is *too narrow*	N	5

a. Cesar Chavez's father was a migrant worker himself. ☐ _____

b. Chavez gained many reforms for migrant workers, but some have been lost. ☐ _____

c. The life of a reformer is never easy. ☐ _____

Score 15 points for each correct answer.   **Score**

Subject Matter   **2**   This passage is primarily concerned with telling about
- ☐ a. unsuccessful reformers.
- ☐ b. the life and work of Cesar Chavez.
- ☐ c. the hard life of a migrant worker.
- ☐ d. how the reforms that Chavez gained were lost.   _____

Supporting Details   **3**   One of Chavez's primary goals was to
- ☐ a. organize migrant workers into a union.
- ☐ b. win a pension for his father.
- ☐ c. build new houses for the workers.
- ☐ d. get the support of Robert F. Kennedy.   _____

Conclusion   **4**   The writer suggests that
- ☐ a. Chavez was not a good organizer.
- ☐ b. migrant workers will soon regain the advantages they have lost.
- ☐ c. Chavez might have had more success if he had a better education.
- ☐ d. reformers like Chavez fail as often as they succeed.   _____

Clarifying Devices   **5**   A change in tone in the final paragraph is signaled by the word
- ☐ a. Unfortunately.
- ☐ b. slide.
- ☐ c. just.
- ☐ d. confident.   _____

Vocabulary in Context   **6**   In this passage remedy means
- ☐ a. outwit.
- ☐ b. fix.
- ☐ c. medicine.
- ☐ d. destroy.   _____

Add your scores for questions 1–6. Enter the total here and on the graph on page 218.   **Total Score**   _____

80 The World's Longest Rivers

At some 2,300 miles in length, the Mississippi is the longest river in the United States; at some 1,000 miles, the Mackenzie is the longest river in Canada. But these waterways seem <u>minuscule</u> in comparison to the world's two lengthiest rivers, the Nile and the Amazon.

The Nile, which begins in central Africa and flows over 4,100 miles north into the Mediterranean, hosted one of the world's great ancient civilizations along its shores. Placid for most of the year, the Nile used to flood annually, thereby creating, irrigating, and carrying new topsoil to the nearby farmland on which ancient Egypt depended for sustenance. A transportation and food source as well, the river carried various vessels up and down its length, from modest fishing and cargo boats to the magnificent barges of the ruling pharaohs. A journey through the unobstructed part of this waterway today would pass by the splendid Valley of the Kings, where the tombs of many of these ancient monarchs have stood for over 3,000 years.

Great civilizations and intensive settlement are hardly associated with the Amazon, yet this 4,000-mile-long South American river carries about 20 percent of the world's fresh water—more than the Mississippi, Nile, and Yangtze combined. Other statistics are equally astounding. Of its 15,000 tributaries, 17 are over 1,000 miles long, and the river itself is so wide at some points that from its center neither shore can be seen. Each second, the Amazon pours some 55 million gallons of water into the Atlantic; there, at its mouth, stands one island larger than Switzerland. Most important of all, the Amazon irrigates the largest tropical rain forest on earth.

Main Idea 1		Answer	Score
Mark the *main idea*		M	15
Mark the statement that is *too broad*		B	5
Mark the statement that is *too narrow*		N	5

a. The world's longest rivers, the Amazon and the Nile, have little more than length in common. ☐ _____

b. Many countries have very long rivers. ☐ _____

c. The Nile is about 4,100 miles long, and the Amazon is about 4,000 miles long. ☐ _____

Score 15 points for each correct answer. **Score**

Subject Matter   **2**   This passage mostly deals with
- [ ] a. interesting facts about the Amazon and the Nile.
- [ ] b. a history of life along the Amazon and the Nile.
- [ ] c. rivers as important natural resources.
- [ ] d. the longest rivers in several large countries.   _____

Supporting Details   **3**   The Amazon is **not** known for
- [ ] a. its many tributaries.
- [ ] b. its amazing width.
- [ ] c. the amount of water it carries.
- [ ] d. the large cities along its banks.   _____

Conclusion   **4**   The writer suggests that a tour along the Nile today would reveal
- [ ] a. modern irrigation methods.
- [ ] b. monuments from ancient times.
- [ ] c. the poverty of present-day Egyptians.
- [ ] d. many houseboats along its shores.   _____

Clarifying Devices   **5**   The writer talks about the two rivers by
- [ ] a. explaining the history of each.
- [ ] b. telling what makes each unique.
- [ ] c. discussing their importance as trade routes.
- [ ] d. describing the specific land that each passes through.   _____

Vocabulary in Context   **6**   Minuscule means
- [ ] a. very large.
- [ ] b. very small.
- [ ] c. medicine.
- [ ] d. destroy.   _____

Add your scores for questions 1–6. Enter the total here and on the graph on page 218.   **Total Score**   _____

81 Getting a Handle on Time

When it's 10:15 in New York, it's 9:15 in Chicago, 8:15 in Salt Lake City, and 7:15 in San Francisco—isn't it? This consistent and orderly time system, based on a grid of time zones, seems so natural that people rarely give it a moment's thought. So you may find it surprising to learn that prior to the late 1800s each community established its own time—by looking at the sun. When the sun shone directly overhead in Washington, D.C., for example, it was 12:00 noon there; up the road in Philadelphia, however, it was 12:07, and in Boston it was 12:24. To measure time with absolute accuracy, it is necessary to move the clock about one minute for every twelve miles of distance; so according to "sun time" your pocket watch would be slightly incorrect if you ventured only a few miles down the road.

It was not until the <u>advent</u> of widespread railroad travel that a need arose for regularized time. At one point over 300 local times were honored within the country, making it literally impossible for trains to arrive consistently on time everywhere. As a result, in 1883 the continental United States was divided into four time zones, centered on approximately the 75th, 90th, 105th, and 120th meridians of longitude. The standardization resulting from this system proved so helpful that in 1884 the International Meridian Conference applied the same procedure to establish time zones around the world. Thus, if it is 11:07 P.M. in Tuscaloosa, Alabama, a little simple research will quickly determine that in Kuala Lumpur, Malaysia, it is 9:07 A.M.—and not 9:15.

Main Idea	1		
		Answer	**Score**
	Mark the *main idea*	M	15
	Mark the statement that is *too broad*	B	5
	Mark the statement that is *too narrow*	N	5

a. It is hard to measure time exactly. ☐ _____

b. Time was regularized, to everyone's benefit, after railroad travel became commonplace. ☐ _____

c. Before standardization, it was impossible to keep trains on time. ☐ _____

Subject Matter **2** The best alternate title for this passage would be
- [ ] a. Why Time Zones Were Established.
- [ ] b. It's 9:07 in Kuala Lumpur.
- [ ] c. Why Trains Rarely Run on Time.
- [ ] d. Understanding Longitude.

_____

Supporting Details **3** Before the 1880s, each town
- [ ] a. had its own train station.
- [ ] b. had the same time as towns 20 or more miles away.
- [ ] c. believed that a system of regulating time was needed.
- [ ] d. established its own time by the sun.

_____

Conclusion **4** The distance between Washington, D.C., and Philadelphia must be
- [ ] a. more than 75 miles.
- [ ] b. more than 150 miles.
- [ ] c. more than 200 miles.
- [ ] d. more than 300 miles.

_____

Clarifying Devices **5** This passage is organized as
- [ ] a. a personal narrative.
- [ ] b. a problem and a solution.
- [ ] c. a spatial description.
- [ ] d. a persuasive essay.

_____

Vocabulary in Context **6** In this passage <u>advent</u> means
- [ ] a. disagreement.
- [ ] b. confusion.
- [ ] c. arrival.
- [ ] d. disappearance.

_____

Add your scores for questions 1–6. Enter the total here and on the graph on page 219.

Total Score

_____

82 Creating Those Shooting Stars

Gazing into the sky on a hot Fourth of July evening, you probably react with pleasure and sometimes even astonishment at the lovely fireworks spectacle you are witnessing. You may not, however, give too much consideration to the origins, or the makings, of the show.

Opinions differ as to who actually produced the first fireworks; most commonly they are attributed to the ancient Chinese, and the credit for introducing them to Europe is given to 13th-century explorer Marco Polo. The composition of fireworks as it exists today was essentially established by the early 1800s; but more primitive versions of fireworks accompanied weddings, festivals, military victories, and other celebrations for hundreds of years prior to that.

The basic ingredient in all fireworks is what is known as black powder, a mixture of saltpeter, charcoal, and sulfur. This is combined with various coloring and binding agents to make a doughlike substance that is cut into small lumps called stars. The stars, which are very <u>volatile</u>, are packed together with loose black powder, which explodes more slowly, into easily burned containers known as shells. A large shell may hold as many as 100 stars and, depending on how it is packaged, may burst into numerous fireworks when propelled into the air.

Fireworks must be handled with great caution. Since stars may explode if exposed to even static electricity, manufacturers must wear cotton rather than synthetic clothing when they work. Igniting fuses must be timed exactly so that shells don't detonate too close to the ground. Pyrotechnics is a very precise art, and the wise technician maintains a healthy respect for it.

Main Idea	1		
		Answer	Score
Mark the *main idea*		M	15
Mark the statement that is *too broad*		B	5
Mark the statement that is *too narrow*		N	5

a. People have always been fascinated by fireworks. ☐ _____

b. Fireworks have a long history, but their basic structure hasn't changed for almost 200 years. ☐ _____

c. A large fireworks shell may hold as many as 100 stars. ☐ _____

Score 15 points for each correct answer.   **Score**

Subject Matter   **2**   This passage deals mainly with
  - ☐ a. the making of fireworks.
  - ☐ b. a history of gunpowder.
  - ☐ c. dangers associated with explosives.
  - ☐ d. how Marco Polo brought a Chinese invention to Europe.   _____

Supporting Details   **3**   The basic ingredient in fireworks is called
  - ☐ a. saltpeter.
  - ☐ b. black powder.
  - ☐ c. stars.
  - ☐ d. shells.   _____

Conclusion   **4**   We can assume that before 1800
  - ☐ a. people did not enjoy fireworks.
  - ☐ b. fireworks were made differently than they are today.
  - ☐ c. fireworks were used mostly for sad occasions.
  - ☐ d. people did not know that fireworks could be dangerous.   _____

Clarifying Devices   **5**   The writer points out the dangers of fireworks by
  - ☐ a. relating a short incident.
  - ☐ b. comparing older fireworks with present-day ones.
  - ☐ c. giving some examples of things to be careful of.
  - ☐ d. listing the ingredients that go into them.   _____

Vocabulary in Context   **6**   In this passage, <u>volatile</u> means
  - ☐ a. time-consuming.
  - ☐ b. able to reach great heights.
  - ☐ c. slow to explode.
  - ☐ d. quick to explode.   _____

Add your scores for questions 1–6. Enter the total here and on the graph on page 219.   **Total Score**   _____

83 Cold or Flu?

Every winter, at least in cold climates, people sink into an all-too-familiar round of illness, with sneezing, sore throat, and stuffed-up head a few of the most common symptoms. Sometimes other conditions, such as a severe cough, are also present, and people wonder whether they have simply caught a cold or are suffering from flu. Since the two illnesses have several common characteristics, the confusion is understandable. Colds are generally rather mild annoyances, but flu can be quite serious and lead to pneumonia. So it is wise to be aware of the differences.

Sneezing, stuffy nose, and sore throat are the most common symptoms of colds, and they are often, but not always, present with flu as well. Chest discomfort and coughing may also accompany both ailments, but in flu they have a tendency to become severe, with heavy, hacking coughing and sometimes bronchitis that may last for weeks afterward.

The symptoms particularly distinguishing flu, which are rarely if ever present with the common cold, are headache, high fever, aches and pains all over the body, a general weakness, and exhaustion. Often the illness begins with vague body pains and headache, then quickly escalates as the victim's bodily temperature becomes <u>elevated</u> and extreme fatigue sets in. Sufferers may find themselves in bed for several days, sleeping much of the time and battling temperatures of 102–104 degrees. Waking moments may be spent coughing uncontrollably.

Though there is presently no cure for the common cold, antibiotics can counteract certain strains of flu. And getting a flu shot at the beginning of each season is a particularly good idea.

Main Idea   1

	Answer	Score
Mark the *main idea*	M	15
Mark the statement that is *too broad*	B	5
Mark the statement that is *too narrow*	N	5

a. There are several cold-weather illnesses. ☐ _____

b. Temperatures as high as 102 degrees are not uncommon with flu. ☐ _____

c. Cold and flu have many similarities but also several differences. ☐ _____

Score 15 points for each correct answer. Score

Subject Matter 2 The information in this passage is mostly about
☐ a. how people catch colds and flu.
☐ b. ways to prevent colds and flu.
☐ c. symptoms of colds and flu.
☐ d. why people are more likely to get sick in winter. _____

Supporting Details 3 Which of the following is **not** a common symptom of a cold?
☐ a. headache
☐ b. coughing
☐ c. sneezing
☐ d. sore throat _____

Conclusion 4 This passage suggests that
☐ a. colds may lead to more serious ailments.
☐ b. flu may lead to more serious ailments.
☐ c. there will soon be a cure for colds.
☐ d. people can avoid getting colds if they are careful. _____

Clarifying Devices 5 The writer develops the ideas in this passage by
☐ a. explaining a process.
☐ b. comparing and contrasting.
☐ c. giving evidence to persuade the reader.
☐ d. relating a short incident. _____

Vocabulary in Context 6 As used in this passage, <u>elevated</u> means
☐ a. a kind of city train.
☐ b. related to the peak of a mountain.
☐ c. high.
☐ d. depressed. _____

Add your scores for questions 1–6. Enter the total here and on the graph on page 219. Total Score _____

84 Proving Fermat's Last Theorem

It was the most tantalizing statement in higher mathematics, and it had been hastily scribbled into the margin of a book. Elementary school students learn the Pythagorean theorem, which is related to it, that $a^2 + b^2 = c^2$. The statement in the margin, however, was a negative, that $a^3 + b^3$ does *not* equal c^3, and that, furthermore, the equation is just as invalid in any situation where the exponent is above 2. So $a^4 + b^4$ never equals c^4, $a^5 + b^5$ never equals c^5, and so on.

The marginal statement had been left by eminent 17th-century mathematician Pierre de Fermat, and it contended that he had discovered a proof for his conjecture— but that there was not enough room to write it in the margin. Fermat's statement intrigued and challenged mathematicians for the next 300 years, for no one could prove it. In higher mathematics, it is not sufficient merely to state that a theorem is true even if it holds true for every number that you try it with; you must devise a proof that can be demonstrated to work with *any* possible number inserted into the equation. A statement has little or no value until such a proof is substantiated.

Fermat's Last Theorem, as it was called, was the most significant unproved theorem in higher mathematics, and it was not conclusively demonstrated to be true until 1994. At that time mathematician Andrew Wiles, who had spent years struggling with the problem, corrected his earlier 1993 proof, and his astonished colleagues certified his work as legitimate.

At 150 pages, however, Wiles's proof is certainly not the same one Fermat envisioned centuries ago. In that respect, Fermat's marginal note will remain an enigma forever.

Main Idea 1

	Answer	Score
Mark the *main idea*	M	15
Mark the statement that is *too broad*	B	5
Mark the statement that is *too narrow*	N	5

a. Many mathematical theorems are difficult to prove. ☐ _____

b. Fermat's famous theorem was not absolutely proved for hundreds of years. ☐ _____

c. Fermat's theorem was that $a^3 + b^3$ does not equal c^3. ☐ _____

Subject Matter   **2**   This passage is mostly concerned with
- ☐ a. why mathematical proofs fascinate some people.
- ☐ b. the life of Pierre de Fermat.
- ☐ c. Fermat's theorem and the difficulties of proving it.
- ☐ d. how Andrew Wiles proved Fermat's theorem. _____

Supporting Details   **3**   Fermat's theorem was not proved for
- ☐ a. 200 years.
- ☐ b. 300 years.
- ☐ c. 400 years.
- ☐ d. 500 years. _____

Conclusion   **4**   It seems logical to assume that Andrew Wiles
- ☐ a. loved a challenge.
- ☐ b. was very arrogant.
- ☐ c. was disliked by his colleagues.
- ☐ d. came up with the same proof that Fermat had in mind. _____

Clarifying Devices   **5**   The writer helps the reader to understand Fermat's theorem by
- ☐ a. comparing it to the Pythagorean theorem.
- ☐ b. showing how Andrew Wiles proved it.
- ☐ c. telling about the famous marginal note.
- ☐ d. explaining why theorems must be proved. _____

Vocabulary in Context   **6**   The word <u>enigma</u> means
- ☐ a. proof.
- ☐ b. theorem.
- ☐ c. untruth.
- ☐ d. mystery. _____

Add your scores for questions 1–6. Enter the total here and on the graph on page 219.   **Total Score** _____

85 The Graveyard of Elephants

Fortune hunters used to think that if they could find the elephants' graveyard they would be rich. Legend had it that old elephants, when they knew they were approaching death, would go to the same secret spot in the jungle to die. According to some accounts, an animal that was wounded or sick would be guided and half carried by other elephants so that it could reach this sacred spot. Of course, if this were true, it would mean that great amounts of ivory would have accumulated at this hidden place. However, despite numerous attempts, no one has ever found this mysterious elephant graveyard.

Recently, however, people have become more interested in learning the truths about live elephants' behavior than in developing fantastic <u>schemes</u> for finding the tusks of dead ones. Interested scientists who have journeyed to Africa have watched elephants in the wild for years, allowing the huge animals to get used to them so they could observe their behavior at close range. What they have learned about elephants is far more exciting than the location of some secret burial site. Researchers have found that elephants are very intelligent and social animals that form strong friendships among themselves and help to defend and raise each other's calves. The sympathetic elephants that crowd around one of their wounded friends are actually trying to nurse and protect it, not lead it off to some mythical graveyard.

Main Idea   1

	Answer	Score
Mark the *main idea*	M	15
Mark the statement that is *too broad*	B	5
Mark the statement that is *too narrow*	N	5

a. Today, people are more interested in learning about live elephants than in finding the mythical elephant graveyard. ☐ _____

b. Fortune hunters, hearing the legend, have tried to find the elephants' graveyard. ☐ _____

c. There are many false legends about animals. ☐ _____

Subject Matter   **2**   This passage focuses mostly on
- ☐ a. fortune hunters.
- ☐ b. elephant legends.
- ☐ c. facts about elephants.
- ☐ d. dead elephants.

            _____

Supporting Details   **3**   According to legends about the elephant graveyard,
- ☐ a. elephants lived there from time to time.
- ☐ b. elephants were not the only animals who went there.
- ☐ c. other elephants helped to carry wounded elephants to the graveyard.
- ☐ d. the graveyard was once a well-known spot.

            _____

Conclusion   **4**   From this passage, we can infer that the writer
- ☐ a. is disappointed that the legend is not true.
- ☐ b. thinks that elephants are cute and cuddly.
- ☐ c. has sympathy for people who believe in the elephant graveyard.
- ☐ d. thinks live elephants are much more interesting than dead ones.

            _____

Clarifying Devices   **5**   The writer contrasts the behavior of fortune hunters with that of
- ☐ a. those who are truly interested in elephants.
- ☐ b. dying elephants.
- ☐ c. other jungle adventurers.
- ☐ d. elephant hunters.

            _____

Vocabulary in Context   **6**   The best substitute for the word <u>schemes</u> in this passage would be
- ☐ a. plans.
- ☐ b. expeditions.
- ☐ c. trails.
- ☐ d. stories.

            _____

Add your scores for questions 1–6. Enter the total here and on the graph on page 219.   **Total Score**   _____

86 The Great Battle for Quebec

For three months the English general James Wolfe had attacked the French forces defending the Canadian city of Quebec. Located on the banks of the mighty St. Lawrence River, Quebec controlled the shipping on this broad waterway that leads to the Great Lakes and the heart of the North American continent. France and Great Britain were competing for control of the American colonies in the Seven Years War of 1756–1763, and the <u>key</u> to an English victory was the conquest of Quebec and access to the St. Lawrence.

In a final desperate attempt, Wolfe decided to circle around the French forces and attack them from the rear. To do this, he had to cross the river, defeat a small group of French guards without allowing them to alarm the nearby French troops, and then get his army of 4,000 men, with their weapons and equipment, up the cliffs known as the Plains of Abraham—all in a single dark night.

On September 13, 1759, the sun rose on an English army that had seemingly miraculously relocated itself to the rear of the French forces. A fierce battle followed, ending with both Wolfe and the French commander, Montcalm, dead on the field. But Wolfe's departing words, as the outcome of the battle became apparent, were "I die contented." Montcalm, when he realized that he too was dying, cried, "Thank God I shall not live to see the surrender of Quebec."

Main Idea 1

	Answer	Score
Mark the *main idea*	M	15
Mark the statement that is *too broad*	B	5
Mark the statement that is *too narrow*	N	5

a. Both France and England wanted the American colonies. ☐ _____

b. General Wolfe attacked the French army that was defending Quebec. ☐ _____

c. The English won the battle for Quebec, the decisive battle of the Seven Years War. ☐ _____

Subject Matter **2** This passage focuses on
- ☐ a. two great generals.
- ☐ b. the Seven Years War of 1756–1763.
- ☐ c. the battle for Quebec.
- ☐ d. the Plains of Abraham.

_____

Supporting Details **3** According to the passage, Wolfe was
- ☐ a. cool and collected.
- ☐ b. anxious to conquer Quebec.
- ☐ c. apathetic to the war's cause.
- ☐ d. not a very good general.

_____

Conclusion **4** We can infer from the passage that
- ☐ a. this battle had no effect on the American colonies.
- ☐ b. Wolfe's plan was successful.
- ☐ c. Montcalm was a bad general.
- ☐ d. the sun's position suddenly changed.

_____

Clarifying Devices **5** The writer reveals the result of the battle by
- ☐ a. quoting the last words of the opposing commanders.
- ☐ b. implying that God was on the side of the English.
- ☐ c. presenting the entire passage from the English point of view.
- ☐ d. relying on the reader's knowledge of history.

_____

Vocabulary in Context **6** In this passage the word <u>key</u> means
- ☐ a. a device for opening a lock.
- ☐ b. essential element.
- ☐ c. a musical pitch.
- ☐ d. a legend on a map.

_____

Add your scores for questions 1–6. Enter the total here and on the graph on page 219.

Total Score

_____

87 A Universal Language

Perhaps you are familiar with the Biblical story of the Tower of Babel, in which humans were punished for their arrogance by having their one language transformed into hundreds of different tongues. Regardless of the origins of our various languages, trying to develop one that could be universally understood has been an obsession to which various people have devoted their lives.

Beginning to examine the problem in the 1500s, philosophers and language experts concluded that it was possible to find an underlying logic that made all languages basically similar. From that point on, scholars began to search for that logic and construct their own languages.

One of the most successful of these artificial languages is called Esperanto. The brainchild of a Polish eye doctor named Zamenhof, Esperanto uses words and grammatical structures from many European languages. At the same time, however, it aims for simplicity: for example, the basic form of all nouns ends in *o;* the basic form of all adjectives ends in *a.* At the time it was developed, around 1887, interest in created languages had reached a high point, and Zamenhof was assisted by many other scholars and language experts who believed in his cause. Their work produced an artificial tongue that at one point could boast speakers in over ninety countries.

Today, English has pretty much become the universal language that Zamenhof and others dreamed of, and there seems to be less need for made-up forms. But interest in artificial languages persists, particularly on the Internet: not only Esperanto, but lesser-known forms such as Interlingua, Glosa, and Lojban all have their devoted followers.

Main Idea	1	Answer	Score
	Mark the *main idea*	M	15
	Mark the statement that is *too broad*	B	5
	Mark the statement that is *too narrow*	N	5

a. Language study has always fascinated people. ☐ _____

b. People have long desired to develop successful universal languages like Esperanto. ☐ _____

c. Dr. Zamenhof was aided in his work by other scholars and language experts. ☐ _____

Score 15 points for each correct answer.

Score

Subject Matter   **2**   The main purpose of this passage is to tell about
- ☐ a. the development of Esperanto.
- ☐ b. languages on the Internet.
- ☐ c. the life of Dr. Zamenhof.
- ☐ d. the Tower of Babel.

_____

Supporting Details   **3**   Esperanto was developed
- ☐ a. in Biblical times.
- ☐ b. in the 1500s.
- ☐ c. in the early 1800s.
- ☐ d. in the late 1800s.

_____

Conclusion   **4**   For people to begin using a created language, the language has to be
- ☐ a. based on European languages.
- ☐ b. created by doctors and other scholars.
- ☐ c. simple.
- ☐ d. popular with government officials.

_____

Clarifying Devices   **5**   The writer tries to capture the reader's interest by
- ☐ a. beginning with a brief anecdote.
- ☐ b. listing several words from Esperanto.
- ☐ c. telling about Dr. Zamenhof's life.
- ☐ d. mentioning the Internet.

_____

Vocabulary in Context   **6**   The word <u>obsession</u> means
- ☐ a. strong impulse or idea.
- ☐ b. argument.
- ☐ c. meeting place.
- ☐ d. fear.

_____

Add your scores for questions 1–6. Enter the total here and on the graph on page 219.

Total Score

_____

88 Don't Fool Around with Camels!

Most people think of a camel as an obedient beast of burden because it is best known for its ability to carry heavy loads across vast stretches of desert without requiring water. In reality, the camel is considerably more than just the Arabian equivalent of the mule. It also possesses a great amount of intelligence and sensitivity.

Arabs assert that camels are so acutely aware of injustice and ill treatment that a camel owner who punishes one of the beasts too harshly finds it difficult to escape the camel's vengeance. Apparently the animal will remember an injury and wait for an appropriate opportunity to get revenge.

In order to protect themselves from the vengeful beasts, Arabian camel drivers have learned to trick their camels into believing they have achieved revenge. When an Arab realizes that he has excited a camel's rage, he places his own garments on the ground in the animal's path. He arranges the clothing so that it appears to cover a man's body. When the camel recognizes its master's clothing on the ground, it seizes the pile with its teeth, shakes the garments violently, and tramples on them in a frenzy. Eventually, after its anger has subsided, the camel departs, assuming its revenge is complete. Only then does the owner of the garments come out of hiding—safe for the time being thanks to this clever <u>ruse</u>.

Main Idea	1		
		Answer	**Score**
Mark the *main idea*		M	15
Mark the statement that is *too broad*		B	5
Mark the statement that is *too narrow*		N	5

a. Camels are sensitive to injustice and will seek revenge on those who harm them. ☐ _____

b. Camel drivers are often the targets of camels' revenge. ☐ _____

c. Camels are sensitive creatures that are aware of injustice. ☐ _____

Subject Matter   **2**   The best alternate title for this passage would be
☐ a. The Life of a Camel Driver.
☐ b. The Camel's Revenge.
☐ c. In the Desert.
☐ d. The Fearsome Camel.   _____

Supporting Details   **3**   According to the passage, camels
☐ a. never drink water.
☐ b. are always violent.
☐ c. are very sensitive.
☐ d. are rarely used anymore.   _____

Conclusion   **4**   From this passage we can conclude that camels
☐ a. are generally vicious toward their owners.
☐ b. are fairly easily deceived.
☐ c. don't see very well.
☐ d. don't communicate well with each other.   _____

Clarifying Devices   **5**   The writer makes the camel's vengeful behavior clearer to the reader by presenting
☐ a. a well-planned argument.
☐ b. a large variety of examples.
☐ c. some eyewitness accounts.
☐ d. a typical incident.   _____

Vocabulary in Context   **6**   The best definition for the word <u>ruse</u> is
☐ a. a deception or hoax.
☐ b. a joke.
☐ c. a game.
☐ d. a beast of burden.   _____

Add your scores for questions 1–6. Enter the total here and on the graph on page 219.   **Total Score**   _____

89 Disaster

The disaster that would give Johnstown, Pennsylvania, a place in history began when it started to rain on the evening of May 30, 1889. All through the night and continuing all the next day the rain poured down, swelling creeks and rivers and filling the reservoir behind the South Fork Dam to overflowing.

At three o'clock in the afternoon of May 31, the Reverend Brown noticed the first break in the face of the old earthen dam and cried, "God have mercy on the people below!" The breach quickly widened, and the swollen lake of water in the reservoir behind the dam hurled itself into the valley below. The collapse of the dam was so sudden that the water surged downhill in a wall 30 to 40 feet high, crushing and carrying along trees, boulders, buildings, railroad cars—everything in its path. When the flood hit a stone bridge 15 miles downstream in Johnstown, the mass of wreckage jammed into a pile about 70 feet high, creating a treacherous new dam that caused the water racing behind it to rise and spread <u>debris</u> over 30 acres of land. Mercifully, most of the startled local citizenry went to their deaths quickly. They never had the slightest chance to evade a watery fate.

More than 2,000 people were killed in the Johnstown flood, making it the worst flood disaster in North American history—a record no one wants to see surpassed.

	Answer	Score
Main Idea 1		
Mark the *main idea*	M	15
Mark the statement that is *too broad*	B	5
Mark the statement that is *too narrow*	N	5

a. Johnstown, Pennsylvania, was flooded on May 31, 1889. ☐ _____

b. Johnstown, Pennsylvania, was the site of a famous disaster. ☐ _____

c. The worst flood in North American history was caused by a broken dam in Johnstown, Pennsylvania. ☐ _____

Subject Matter   2   This passage is primarily about
- ☐ a. a Memorial Day celebration.
- ☐ b. dam safety measures.
- ☐ c. unusually heavy rainfalls.
- ☐ d. a terrible flood.

_____

Supporting Details   3   The Johnstown flood is famous because of
- ☐ a. the number of lives that were lost.
- ☐ b. the size of the dam that broke.
- ☐ c. the date on which it happened.
- ☐ d. the speed at which the flood moved.

_____

Conclusion   4   What is the most likely reason that no flood has since claimed so many lives?
- ☐ a. People no longer live near dams.
- ☐ b. There are fewer heavy rainfalls.
- ☐ c. Dams are being built more carefully.
- ☐ d. Towns are not built to survive floods.

_____

Clarifying Devices   5   The writer quotes the Reverend Brown in order to
- ☐ a. supply all the facts.
- ☐ b. add emotional impact.
- ☐ c. reveal his own bias.
- ☐ d. support his argument.

_____

Vocabulary in Context   6   <u>Debris</u> is
- ☐ a. chaos.
- ☐ b. disease.
- ☐ c. terror.
- ☐ d. wreckage.

_____

Add your scores for questions 1–6. Enter the total here and on the graph on page 219.   **Total Score**   _____

90 An Unusual Collaboration

The making of a dictionary is a slow, exacting, tedious labor. Lexicographers—dictionary-makers—can't rely on hunches or hearsay in writing definitions; they must carefully collect and evaluate citations, written examples of words in use. It was during the writing and assembling of the Oxford English Dictionary, a massive work over 70 years in the making, that a very unusual collaboration of lexicographer and citation-gatherer occurred.

William Chester Minor, the citation-gatherer, was an American doctor who began to suffer paranoid delusions sometime after serving as a surgeon in the Civil War. One night in London in 1871 he killed an innocent brewery worker who he imagined was pursuing him; for this offense he was committed for life to an asylum for the criminally insane. An intelligent man <u>grappling</u> with a disease with no known cure, he desperately searched for a way to give his life meaning.

James Murray, the lexicographer, was the head of the dictionary project. Needing vast numbers of citations to complete his ambitious work, he assembled a large corps of volunteers to aid him. A friend of Minor's informed him of the project, and the unusual collaboration began.

Minor, with nothing but time on his hands and a strong need to redeem himself, became Murray's most prolific citation writer. For years he read and recorded constantly, producing voluminous files of citations that the dictionary-maker found very valuable.

A grateful Murray eventually learned the true circumstances of Minor's sad existence. Though able to do nothing to help Minor, he befriended him and often visited him in the asylum.

Main Idea	1		
		Answer	Score
Mark the *main idea*		M	15
Mark the statement that is *too broad*		B	5
Mark the statement that is *too narrow*		N	5
a. Need can create strange partnerships.		☐	_____
b. Minor became one of Murray's best citation writers.		☐	_____
c. The unusual collaboration between Murray and Minor produced benefits for each man.		☐	_____

Subject Matter   **2**   The best alternate title for this passage would be
- ☐ a. The Strange Life of James Murray.
- ☐ b. Murray and Minor: Bound by Need.
- ☐ c. The Making of the Oxford English Dictionary.
- ☐ d. The Work of a Citation Writer.

_____

Supporting Details   **3**   Minor was imprisoned for
- ☐ a. murder.
- ☐ b. mental illness.
- ☐ c. hiding his identity.
- ☐ d. practicing medicine without a license.

_____

Conclusion   **4**   Murray let Minor continue to work for him because
- ☐ a. he felt sorry for Minor.
- ☐ b. he believed Minor would soon be released from prison.
- ☐ c. Minor did such good work.
- ☐ d. he was committed to helping the mentally ill.

_____

Clarifying Devices   **5**   The example of "[killing] an innocent brewery worker who he imagined was pursuing him" is used to help explain the term
- ☐ a. collaboration.
- ☐ b. citation gatherer.
- ☐ c. paranoid delusions.
- ☐ d. asylum.

_____

Vocabulary in Context   **6**   Grappling means
- ☐ a. overcoming.
- ☐ b. discovering.
- ☐ c. climbing.
- ☐ d. struggling.

_____

Add your scores for questions 1–6. Enter the total here and on the graph on page 219.   **Total Score** _____

91 Inventions That Almost Didn't Happen

Clever, useful inventions come about because enterprising people look for real needs in society and then develop products that will meet those needs—right? Surprisingly, this is not always true. Some of the most basic, taken-for-granted products in our society exist by accident or because someone made a mistake on the way to developing something else.

For example, in 1970 a man named Spencer Silver, an employee at 3M laboratories, was trying to create a strong new adhesive but came up with a very weak one instead. Four years later one of his colleagues remembered Silver's glue because the paper page markers he inserted into his hymnbook in church one Sunday morning kept falling out. Paper coated with a weak adhesive that stuck to things and yet could easily be removed clearly was a product with great <u>potential</u>. And so the Post-it note was born.

Another fastening agent, usually known by the brand-name Velcro, was developed because its inventor, George de Mestral, noticed that some burrs had accidentally caught on his jacket and were holding it together. De Mestral, an engineer, studied the structure of the burr and, after years of experimenting, came up with his own burr-like fastener.

As a final example, rubber had been around for centuries but had limited use: it melted in high heat and turned brittle in intense cold. Searching for ways to harden it, researcher Charles Goodyear accidentally dropped a rubber-sulfur mixture onto a hot stove, thereby discovering "vulcanization," the process of making rubber firm and flexible.

Main Idea 1

	Answer	Score
Mark the *main idea*	M	15
Mark the statement that is *too broad*	B	5
Mark the statement that is *too narrow*	N	5

a. Many useful products were the result of accidents or mistakes. ☐ _____

b. Many inventors make mistakes. ☐ _____

c. Some accidental inventions are used to fasten things together. ☐ _____

Subject Matter   2   This passage is mainly about
- ☐ a. how Post-it notes were developed.
- ☐ b. the lives of three inventors.
- ☐ c. the cleverness of inventors.
- ☐ d. things that were invented as a result of accidents.

_____

Supporting Details   3   A need for Spencer Silver's adhesive was discovered
- ☐ a. at church one Sunday morning.
- ☐ b. about a month after Silver invented it.
- ☐ c. when a strong, heavy-duty glue was needed.
- ☐ d. by some manufacturers of shoes.

_____

Conclusion   4   We can conclude that most inventors are
- ☐ a. people with little patience.
- ☐ b. people who are interested in how things work.
- ☐ c. relatively young.
- ☐ d. determined to decide on one approach and follow it no matter what.

_____

Clarifying Devices   5   The word "Surprisingly" in the first paragraph introduces
- ☐ a. a contradiction of the preceding sentence.
- ☐ b. a short anecdote.
- ☐ c. an example.
- ☐ d. a persuasive statement.

_____

Vocabulary in Context   6   As used in this passage, <u>potential</u> means
- ☐ a. concern.
- ☐ b. value to collectors.
- ☐ c. promise.
- ☐ d. time.

_____

Add your scores for questions 1–6. Enter the total here and on the graph on page 219.   **Total Score**

_____

92 The Master Forger

The literary giants of the past have always been prey to clever forgers desiring wealth and borrowed fame. One of the most popular targets of forgers has been William Shakespeare. And probably the most successful of all Shakespeare forgers was an 18-year-old boy named William Henry Ireland.

Ireland, the son of a respected book dealer, perpetrated his hoax on the literary public in the late 18th century. The boy's success rested on his astonishing skill both in imitating Shakespeare's style and in producing documents with an appearance of age and authenticity.

Ireland claimed that the works he forged were written by Shakespeare. He based his claim on a deed, supposedly signed by Shakespeare, in which the bard bequeathed certain of his books and papers to a William Henry Ireland, whom young Ireland claimed as an ancestor. His inheritance, the boy revealed, consisted of letters by Shakespeare to his wife, two plays, and legal contracts and receipts signed by the playwright. Outstanding scholars, critics, and poets examined the "finds," and, except for Edmund Malone, the leading Shakespearean expert of the day, all proclaimed them authentic. Richard Sheridan bought the play *Vortigern and Rowena* and produced it with a star cast at his Drury Lane theatre.

The play's presentation helped Malone convince other skeptics of the hoax, and Ireland finally confessed. However, Ireland had the last laugh. The controversy created a market for his phony Shakespearean works, and Ireland seized the opportunity and did a brisk and profitable business making and selling imitations of his imitations.

Main Idea	1		Answer	Score
		Mark the *main idea*	M	15
		Mark the statement that is *too broad*	B	5
		Mark the statement that is *too narrow*	N	5

a. Ireland was a highly successful forger of Shakespearean works and documents. ☐ _____

b. There have been many attempted forgeries of William Shakespeare's works. ☐ _____

c. *Vortigern and Rowena* was a play forged by W. H. Ireland. ☐ _____

Subject Matter   **2**   The passage is primarily about
    ☐ a. William Shakespeare.
    ☐ b. literary forgery.
    ☐ c. the forged play *Vortigern and Rowena*.
    ☐ d. William Henry Ireland's hoax.

_____

Supporting Details   **3**   How did Ireland claim to have received the Shakespearean documents?
    ☐ a. He said he bought them from Richard Sheridan.
    ☐ b. He said they had been deeded to an ancestor and he inherited them.
    ☐ c. He said they were given to him by Edmund Malone.
    ☐ d. He said his father, a book dealer, bought them at an auction.

_____

Conclusion   **4**   We can conclude that Ireland
    ☐ a. did not forge the Shakespearean documents.
    ☐ b. helped his father forge the documents.
    ☐ c. was successful because he was bold.
    ☐ d. had no talent as a playwright or a poet.

_____

Clarifying Devices   **5**   "However, Ireland had the last laugh" means
    ☐ a. most critics still believed Ireland.
    ☐ b. Ireland thought his hoax was funny.
    ☐ c. Ireland had a better sense of humor than his critics.
    ☐ d. Ireland made money from his hoax even after it was discovered.

_____

Vocabulary in Context   **6**   As used in the passage, the word <u>bequeathed</u> means
    ☐ a. sold.
    ☐ b. sent.
    ☐ c. gave.
    ☐ d. offered.

_____

Add your scores for questions 1–6. Enter the total here and on the graph on page 219.

Total Score

_____

93 Discovering a Treasure Worth Billions

For some people unearthing buried treasure is an obsession. However, for others devising the means to locate that treasure is the greater obsession. Tommy Thompson, even though he located a sunken ship carrying as much as $1 billion in gold, definitely belongs in the latter category.

Thompson developed an interest in underwater salvage as a young man. He quickly became determined to find a way to explore deep-sea wrecks. In the mid-1980s, when Thompson began his exploratory forays, no accurate equipment was available. So Thompson and his crew developed their own. They devised a huge remote operating vehicle weighing over 6,000 pounds and equipped it with sonar detectors, cameras, and, most importantly, arms for retrieval of artifacts. So <u>meticulously</u> designed were their equipment and their techniques that they were able to pick up newly minted coins from the ocean floor without scratching them.

The ship that Thompson had set his sights on was the *Central America,* a steamship carrying gold from the mines in California, which had sunk off the South Carolina coast in 1857. Thompson determined the exact whereabouts of the lost ship by interviewing descendants of survivors and poring through written accounts of the tragedy. In September 1988 Thompson and his crew finally found the remains of the *Central America.* Their work not only netted them millions of dollars, but also opened up a whole new era of underwater retrieval.

Main Idea 1

	Answer	Score
Mark the *main idea*	M	15
Mark the statement that is *too broad*	B	5
Mark the statement that is *too narrow*	N	5

a. Tommy Thompson systematically found ways to locate and retrieve the *Central America's* treasure. ☐ _____

b. Tommy Thompson's crew finally discovered the remains of the *Central America* in September 1988. ☐ _____

c. Advanced methods of searching can help treasure seekers find great riches. ☐ _____

Score 15 points for each correct answer.   **Score**

Subject Matter   **2**   An appropriate alternate title for this passage would be

☐ a. Treasures in Deep Waters.
☐ b. Tommy Thompson's Early Career.
☐ c. Tracking Down the *Central America.*
☐ d. New Equipment and Techniques.

_____

Supporting Details   **3**   The kinds of wrecks Thompson was interested in were

☐ a. ships in the Caribbean.
☐ b. pirate ships.
☐ c. ships sunk in deep water.
☐ d. ships with wooden hulls.

_____

Conclusion   **4**   We can conclude that Thompson

☐ a. started out with a great deal of money.
☐ b. lived on a boat for most of the year.
☐ c. had ancestors who had been on the *Central America.*
☐ d. was a skillful inventor.

_____

Clarifying Devices   **5**   In sentence 2, the word "However" could be replaced by

☐ a. But.
☐ b. Therefore.
☐ c. Similarly.
☐ d. Thus.

_____

Vocabulary in Context   **6**   The word <u>meticulously</u> means

☐ a. very slowly.
☐ b. spectacularly.
☐ c. precisely and carefully.
☐ d. humanly.

_____

Add your scores for questions 1–6. Enter the total here and on the graph on page 219.

Total Score

_____

94 The Trail of Tears

During the settlement of America by Europeans, many American Indian groups were driven off lands they had inhabited for generations. One of the most shameful episodes of forced evacuation was of the Cherokee Indians, who were moved from the eastern United States all the way to Oklahoma. This long, bitter journey, during which over 4,000 people died, was known to the Cherokee as "The Trail Where They Cried," or "The Trail of Tears."

Though they had earlier warred with the encroaching European-Americans, by the 1830s the Cherokee in northern Georgia changed their approach and adopted many of the European-Americans' ways. An elected tribal council and a constitution similar to that of the United States replaced the old clan system of government. People dressed as the European-Americans did and changed from hunters to growers, living on prosperous farms with cultivated fields and large herds of livestock. But <u>acquiescence</u> to European-American customs did not appease the nearby settlers, who looked jealously at the rich Cherokee land—especially after gold was discovered there.

In 1835 some 300 Cherokee, frustrated by European-Americans ignoring their laws, agreed to give up their land for $5 million and move to Oklahoma. Though the vast majority of Cherokee petitioned the U.S. government to overturn this agreement, their fate was sealed. Between 1838 and 1839, about 17,000 Cherokee were forcibly moved—some dying of measles or dysentery along the way, others stranded without provisions over a harsh winter. The lives and livelihoods of this proud, peaceable people were destroyed.

Main Idea	1	Answer	Score
	Mark the *main idea*	M	15
	Mark the statement that is *too broad*	B	5
	Mark the statement that is *too narrow*	N	5

a. Adapting to the European-Americans' ways did not keep the Cherokee from being driven thousands of miles from their home. ☐ _____

b. Gold was a motive in driving the Cherokee from their land. ☐ _____

c. Many American Indian groups were forced off their lands. ☐ _____

Subject Matter **2** Another good title for this passage would be
- [ ] a. The Results of Poverty.
- [ ] b. American Indian Life in the 1830s.
- [ ] c. A History of the Cherokee.
- [ ] d. A Great Injustice.

_____

Supporting Details **3** By the 1830s the Cherokee in northern Georgia worked as
- [ ] a. hunters.
- [ ] b. farmers.
- [ ] c. horse trainers.
- [ ] d. government inspectors.

_____

Conclusion **4** The attitude of the U.S. government toward the Cherokee was that
- [ ] a. the government wanted to take the Cherokees' land.
- [ ] b. the Cherokee would find prosperity in Oklahoma.
- [ ] c. the Cherokee should be punished for waging war.
- [ ] d. European-Americans should be fair to the Cherokee.

_____

Clarifying Devices **5** As used in the passage, words like "shameful" and "bitter" suggest that the writer
- [ ] a. sympathizes with the Cherokee.
- [ ] b. sympathizes with the European-Americans.
- [ ] c. thinks that both sides were wrong.
- [ ] d. wants to amuse the reader.

_____

Vocabulary in Context **6** The word <u>acquiescence</u> means
- [ ] a. a disagreement.
- [ ] b. a giving in.
- [ ] c. an act of revenge.
- [ ] d. a telling of lies.

_____

Add your scores for questions 1–6. Enter the total here and on the graph on page 219.   **Total Score**

_____

95 The Work of the WPA

The Great Depression that followed the stock market crash of 1929 saw hundreds of thousands of Americans out of work. In this era of great fear and despair, citizens looked desperately to the federal government for assistance. Of all the programs devised by President Roosevelt when he took office in 1932, few were more criticized—or had more lasting impact—than the Work Projects Administration, better known as the WPA.

The intent of the WPA, which functioned from 1935 to 1943, was to devise and administer public works projects to help relieve unemployment. The majority of these projects involved historic or artistic endeavors. The WPA's Writers Project, for example, was responsible not only for such practical works as state guidebooks but also for the compilation of historically valuable oral histories. Over 2,900 of these records were collected in 24 states. They provide an irreplaceable firsthand account of people's diets, customs, celebrations, and political and religious beliefs at the time.

The artworks created through the Federal Arts Project are one of the WPA's most lasting achievements. Out-of-work painters, both famous and unknown, created murals that beautified schools, libraries, and government buildings. WPA photographers traveled across the country recording the hardships of life on small rural farms. When the United States entered World War II, WPA artists were enlisted to produce posters supporting the war effort. Many WPA artworks, including hundreds of small drawings depicting scenes of everyday life, still exist today.

Main Idea	1		Answer	Score
	Mark the *main idea*		M	15
	Mark the statement that is *too broad*		B	5
	Mark the statement that is *too narrow*		N	5

a. Government intervention can often help in times of crisis. ☐ _____

b. WPA artists painted murals in schools and libraries. ☐ _____

c. The WPA produced many valuable and lasting works. ☐ _____

Subject Matter   **2**   The passage is mainly about
- ☐ a. projects undertaken by the WPA.
- ☐ b. the effect of the Great Depression on the United States.
- ☐ c. how oral histories help us understand Americans of the period.
- ☐ d. WPA artists and photographers.   _____

Supporting Details   **3**   WPA photographers tried to
- ☐ a. create artistic works that could hang in museums.
- ☐ b. record the hard life on American farms.
- ☐ c. show the beauty of the natural landscape.
- ☐ d. help the war effort.   _____

Conclusion   **4**   This passage suggests that the WPA
- ☐ a. trained artists before it sent them out to work.
- ☐ b. had several smaller organizations working within it.
- ☐ c. was President Roosevelt's favorite project.
- ☐ d. will some day be reorganized and help people again.   _____

Clarifying Devices   **5**   The author develops this passage mainly through
- ☐ a. a narrative about a WPA worker.
- ☐ b. comparison and contrast.
- ☐ c. a persuasive argument.
- ☐ d. examples.   _____

Vocabulary in Context   **6**   The word <u>compilation</u> means
- ☐ a. distribution.
- ☐ b. separation.
- ☐ c. collection.
- ☐ d. resignation.   _____

Add your scores for questions 1–6. Enter the total here and on the graph on page 219.   **Total Score**   _____

96 Ballooning: Transportation or Competition?

From earliest times human beings have looked to the sky and wished to soar through it like the birds. Pioneer airmen Wilbur and Orville Wright <u>launched</u> the modern Aviation Age with their motor-powered plane in 1903, but some 140 years earlier daredevils had begun leaving the earth via balloons, in an alternate version of flying that still persists today.

The first manned balloon took to the sky in France in 1783—after its inventors had safely tested their device with a sheep, rooster, and duck as passengers. Though that hot-air-filled balloon remained aloft only 20 minutes and traveled a mere five miles, within two years balloonists had traversed the 30-mile-wide English Channel. In 1793 the first balloon went up in America, a hydrogen-filled device whose take-off was observed by George Washington himself.

Once airplanes had replaced balloons as the principal means of air transportation, balloonists concentrated on setting height, distance, and duration records. In the 1970s and 1980s several transoceanic records were set and broken. These feats were made possible because of new techniques for keeping balloons—now generally helium-filled—at steady temperatures.

But circumnavigating the globe remained the final, elusive target until March 1999. After a 19-day flight, Bertrand Piccard of Switzerland and Brian Jones of England landed in Egypt, having flown 29,056 miles to circle the globe. At times they flew at more than 36,000 feet and over 114 miles per hour.

Main Idea   1

	Answer	Score
Mark the *main idea*	M	15
Mark the statement that is *too broad*	B	5
Mark the statement that is *too narrow*	N	5

    a. People began flying in balloons in 1783. ☐ _____

    b. Human beings have always had the desire to fly. ☐ _____

    c. Once a method for transportation, ballooning is now primarily a sport. ☐ _____

Subject Matter   **2**   The purpose of this passage is mainly to provide
☐ a. a comparison between airplanes and balloons.
☐ b. information about the life of Steve Fossett.
☐ c. a short history of ballooning.
☐ d. a list of ballooning records.   _____

Supporting Details   **3**   The first manned balloon flight was
☐ a. in America.
☐ b. over a field in France.
☐ c. over the English Channel.
☐ d. across the Atlantic.   _____

Conclusion   **4**   This passage suggests that flying in a balloon has always required
☐ a. luck.
☐ b. money.
☐ c. guts.
☐ d. fear.   _____

Clarifying Devices   **5**   The information in this passage is presented
☐ a. through a series of anecdotes.
☐ b. by means of several descriptions of balloons.
☐ c. in rough chronological order.
☐ d. as a series of questions and answers.   _____

Vocabulary in Context   **6**   In this passage <u>launched</u> means
☐ a. set afloat.
☐ b. started.
☐ c. caused argument over.
☐ d. refused.   _____

Add your scores for questions 1–6. Enter the total here and on the graph on page 219.   **Total Score**   _____

97 Life in a Biosphere

Drawings of human colonies on other planets often picture the entire community under a glass or plastic bubble. The bubble is intended to create an atmosphere with adequate oxygen and other essential elements. But similar bubblelike structures have also been constructed on earth. One of the most famous, and controversial, is a site in the Arizona desert.

Biosphere 2, as it is called, was built not far from Tucson in 1984 and is now run by Columbia University. This huge (7,200,000-cubic-foot) glass and steel construction contains several separate ecosystems, including a desert, a rain forest, and a 900,000-gallon "ocean." The climactic conditions—humidity, temperature, air quality—are regulated by sensors and can be adjusted as needed or desired. For example, a rainstorm can be created to increase the humidity. These adjustable features of Biosphere 2 make it an ideal location to perform experiments to help determine the effects of such climactic changes as global warming.

The current conditions at Biosphere 2 are vastly different from those in 1993, when eight people who had moved into the environment with great fanfare two years earlier moved out in failure. Though promising to be self-sufficient, these "colonists" had so much trouble regulating the environment that they reportedly had food smuggled in to them. Oxygen levels became dangerously low; most plants and animals died. In taking over the unsuccessful site, Columbia hopes to erase its <u>notorious</u> past by focusing on small research projects that gradually answer some of Biosphere 1's—that is, Earth's—most basic environmental questions.

Main Idea	1		
		Answer	**Score**
	Mark the *main idea*	M	15
	Mark the statement that is *too broad*	B	5
	Mark the statement that is *too narrow*	N	5

    a. Controlled environments are a challenge to maintain. ☐ _____

    b. Earlier colonists at Biosphere 2 were unsuccessful. ☐ _____

    c. Biosphere 2 is a controlled environment with a controversial past. ☐ _____

Score 15 points for each correct answer.   Score

Subject Matter 2 This passage primarily deals with
- ☐ a. conditions of life in Biosphere 2.
- ☐ b. building controlled environments on other planets.
- ☐ c. why Biosphere 2 failed in the past.
- ☐ d. what makes a good biosphere colonist.

_____

Supporting Details 3 Biosphere 2 is now run by
- ☐ a. a group of eight colonists.
- ☐ b. Columbia University.
- ☐ c. the city of Tucson.
- ☐ d. scientists who hope to establish Biosphere 3.

_____

Conclusion 4 The passage suggests that earlier colonists of Biosphere 2
- ☐ a. did not like living in a controlled environment.
- ☐ b. found it very difficult to live in a controlled environment.
- ☐ c. still are involved with Biosphere 2.
- ☐ d. have now left the country in disgrace.

_____

Clarifying Devices 5 The writer helps you understand what Biosphere 2 is like by
- ☐ a. comparing its features with those of an outer space biosphere.
- ☐ b. explaining the process by which it was constructed.
- ☐ c. referring to an interview with one of the former inhabitants.
- ☐ d. describing its appearance and conditions.

_____

Vocabulary in Context 6 In this passage <u>notorious</u> means
- ☐ a. well known for something good.
- ☐ b. well known for something bad.
- ☐ c. dangerous.
- ☐ d. interesting.

_____

Add your scores for questions 1–6. Enter the total here and on the graph on page 219.   Total Score

_____

98 Missing and Presumed Dead

The violent overthrow of governments by revolution, especially when the assassination of royalty is involved, often leads to remarkable myths. Romantic stories about survivors begin circulating almost immediately, put forth either by supporters of the deceased royalty or by individuals claiming to be family members who have miraculously escaped. Two of the longest-lived survivor myths involve Louis XVII of France and Anastasia, daughter of Russian czar Nicholas II.

Louis XVII, the dauphin (heir to the throne) of France, was only seven when his father was beheaded by supporters of the Revolution in 1793. Strong evidence exists that the young boy died in prison of tuberculosis two years later; in fact, his uncle assumed the throne in 1814. But for at least 50 years afterward stories about the "lost dauphin" circulated widely. One claimed that after his father's death Louis was put in the care of a shoemaker and eventually smuggled into America. Over 30 individuals at times claimed to be the dauphin, including a priest who died near Green Bay, Wisconsin, but none of these claims was ever substantiated.

The Anastasia story is equally bizarre. In July 1918 the entire family of Czar Nicholas II of Russia was assassinated by Bolshevik revolutionaries in Siberia. Almost immediately rumors began that the youngest daughter, 17-year-old Anastasia, had been spared, and pretenders began to <u>proliferate</u>: one, a woman named Anna Anderson, claimed to be Anastasia until her death in 1984. But DNA testing has laid this story to rest: Anderson was proven to be a fraud, and the remains of all of Nicholas's children were found and identified at the assassination site.

Main Idea	1		
		Answer	**Score**
	Mark the *main idea*	M	15
	Mark the statement that is *too broad*	B	5
	Mark the statement that is *too narrow*	N	5

a. Louis XVII of France and Anastasia of Russia were two so-called missing heirs. ☐ _____

b. Many people like to pretend that they are lost royalty. ☐ _____

c. Anastasia's father was Czar Nicholas II. ☐ _____

Subject Matter   **2**   Another appropriate title for this passage would be
- ☐ a. Violent European Royalty.
- ☐ b. Two Lost Heirs.
- ☐ c. The French and Russian Revolutions.
- ☐ d. The Uncovering of a Hoax.

_____

Supporting Details   **3**   There is evidence that the Dauphin of France died
- ☐ a. by beheading.
- ☐ b. of tuberculosis.
- ☐ c. in an American jail.
- ☐ d. when he was 50 years old.

_____

Conclusion   **4**   This passage suggests that with DNA testing
- ☐ a. there will be fewer false claims to thrones.
- ☐ b. it will be possible to tell the exact month that someone died.
- ☐ c. no crimes will go unpunished.
- ☐ d. contagious diseases will be detected earlier.

_____

Clarifying Devices   **5**   The expression "laid this story to rest" in the final paragraph refers to
- ☐ a. Anna Anderson's death.
- ☐ b. Anastasia's death.
- ☐ c. taking a story out of circulation for a time.
- ☐ d. the end of an untrue story.

_____

Vocabulary in Context   **6**   The word <u>proliferate</u> means
- ☐ a. be denied.
- ☐ b. answer roughly.
- ☐ c. wear a disguise.
- ☐ d. spread widely.

_____

Add your scores for questions 1–6. Enter the total here and on the graph on page 219.   **Total Score**

_____

99 Hearing Hazards

Pardon me? As you get older, you may notice that your hearing is not as sharp as it once was. Although age does affect hearing, hearing loss is most likely to occur because of exposure to constant sounds in one's daily life.

The American Speech and Hearing Association has estimated that 40 million Americans are subjected every day to dangerously high levels of noise. Sound is measured in decibels, and studies show that permanent hearing <u>impairment</u> can result from exposure to sound levels of about 85 decibels. Many high decibel noises come from machines, but machines are not the only producers of painfully loud noises. A screaming baby, at 90 decibels, is more damaging to the sensitive inner ear than a vacuum cleaner at 70 decibels, street traffic at 75 decibels, or an alarm clock at 80. Prolonged exposure to the blare of a jackhammer, whose noise level reaches 100 decibels, a power mower at 105 decibels, an auto horn at 120 decibels, or a jet engine at 140 decibels can cause permanent damage to a person's hearing.

Obviously, people such as airplane pilots or construction workers, who are regularly exposed to loud noises, should take precautions to protect their hearing. A survey done by the New York League for the Hard of Hearing clearly points up one of these occupational hazards. The study indicates that 50 percent of all rock disc jockeys have suffered hearing damage, and of these 33 percent have become partially deaf.

Main Idea 1

	Answer	Score
Mark the *main idea*	M	15
Mark the statement that is *too broad*	B	5
Mark the statement that is *too narrow*	N	5

a. Noises in our everyday lives may cause hearing damage. ☐ _____

b. Many occupations have hidden dangers. ☐ _____

c. Loud machine noises often cause damage to hearing. ☐ _____

Score 15 points for each correct answer.   **Score**

Subject Matter   **2**   This passage is mostly about
- ☐ a. how sound is measured.
- ☐ b. the effect of loud noises on hearing.
- ☐ c. the sensitivity of the inner ear.
- ☐ d. the effect of sound on disc jockeys.   _____

Supporting Details   **3**   According to the passage, airplane pilots should be concerned about their hearing because
- ☐ a. most pilots suffer hearing loss.
- ☐ b. high altitudes put pressure on the ear.
- ☐ c. jet engines can cause hearing damage.
- ☐ d. noise levels in airport terminals are hazardous.   _____

Conclusion   **4**   We can conclude from the passage that
- ☐ a. most jet pilots become deaf.
- ☐ b. hearing loss is more likely to be caused by old age than by high noise levels.
- ☐ c. 40 million Americans have suffered permanent damage to their hearing.
- ☐ d. someone employed as a jackhammer operator may suffer permanent hearing loss.   _____

Clarifying Devices   **5**   The writer mentions that a study showed that "50 percent of all rock disc jockeys have suffered hearing damage" in order to
- ☐ a. show that rock may be more harmful than other types of music.
- ☐ b. disprove claims that rock music has safe decibel levels.
- ☐ c. show that certain occupations have high levels of noise that can cause hearing loss.
- ☐ d. get an emotional response from the reader.   _____

Vocabulary in Context   **6**   The word <u>impairment</u> is closest in meaning to
- ☐ a. sensitivity.
- ☐ b. change.
- ☐ c. improvement.
- ☐ d. damage.   _____

Add your scores for questions 1–6. Enter the total here and on the graph on page 219.   **Total Score**   _____

100 A Short Career

With his expressive style and subtly mysterious imagery, Jean Nicholas Arthur Rimbaud, the nineteenth-century Frenchman known as the Father of the Symbolist movement, had an unquestionably profound effect on modern poetry. The older poet Verlaine, greatly influenced by Rimbaud, drew critical attention to him. This helped place the young man at the head of the new literary movement that was stirring in France.

But Rimbaud seems to have had little desire to lead the way. In fact his life as a poet lasted only from the time he was 15 until he was 20. He spent his early twenties wandering through Europe in drunken debauchery, often ill or acutely poverty-stricken, and apparently writing nothing to fulfill the brilliant promise of his teens. Finally renouncing his art completely, Rimbaud traveled to North Africa and became manager of a trading station, exporting coffee, gum, and ivory and engaging in the profitable traffic of arms and ammunition.

Scholars are certain that Rimbaud was aware of his growing renown in Europe, which resulted from the publication, in his absence, of his poetic collection *Illuminations*. Enthusiasts in France wrote to him, requesting his return to head the Symbolist movement. His choice was to stay in Ethiopia.

Rimbaud died at the age of 37, having written nothing since his 20th birthday. His poetry continues to be the <u>focus</u> of critical attention and admiration and is still a model for poets, despite the fact that it was written by a teenage boy.

Main Idea	1		Answer	Score
	Mark the *main idea*		M	15
	Mark the statement that is *too broad*		B	5
	Mark the statement that is *too narrow*		N	5
	a. Rimbaud gave up poetry for business.		☐	_____
	b. Young poets such as Rimbaud have influenced generations of poets.		☐	_____
	c. Rimbaud wrote brilliant poetry as a teenager but ultimately rejected his art and fame.		☐	_____

Subject Matter   **2**   This passage is mostly about Rimbaud's
     ☐ a. influence on the Symbolist poets.
     ☐ b. poetic style.
     ☐ c. life and career.
     ☐ d. debt to Verlaine.   _____

Supporting Details   **3**   According to the passage, while Rimbaud was in North Africa, his fame grew in Europe because
     ☐ a. a collection of his poems was published.
     ☐ b. Verlaine told critics about him.
     ☐ c. he sent his poetry to enthusiasts in France.
     ☐ d. the Symbolists were using his poetry as a model.   _____

Conclusion   **4**   The last paragraph of the passage implies that
     ☐ a. Rimbaud's poetry is noteworthy because it was written by a teenager.
     ☐ b. Rimbaud's poetry is less critically acclaimed than it was in his lifetime.
     ☐ c. it is surprising that a teenager's work was good enough to have had such a lasting value and influence.
     ☐ d. Rimbaud's work does not deserve the attention and admiration it receives.   _____

Clarifying Devices   **5**   The writer develops the story by
     ☐ a. describing Rimbaud's poetry.
     ☐ b. comparing Rimbaud to Verlaine.
     ☐ c. recalling other people's descriptions of Rimbaud.
     ☐ d. telling facts about Rimbaud's life.   _____

Vocabulary in Context   **6**   As used in this passage, a <u>focus</u> is
     ☐ a. a point of attraction.
     ☐ b. one of the points in an ellipse.
     ☐ c. the spot where everything is clear.
     ☐ d. the starting place of an earthquake.   _____

Add your scores for questions 1–6. Enter the total here and on the graph on page 219.   **Total Score**   _____

Answer Key

Passage 1:	1a. **M**	1b. **N**	1c. **B**	2. **a**	3. **d**	4. **a**	5. **b**	6. **d**
Passage 2:	1a. **M**	1b. **B**	1c. **N**	2. **c**	3. **d**	4. **b**	5. **a**	6. **b**
Passage 3:	1a. **N**	1b. **M**	1c. **B**	2. **c**	3. **c**	4. **c**	5. **b**	6. **c**
Passage 4:	1a. **M**	1b. **N**	1c. **B**	2. **a**	3. **c**	4. **d**	5. **b**	6. **c**
Passage 5:	1a. **M**	1b. **N**	1c. **B**	2. **b**	3. **c**	4. **c**	5. **d**	6. **b**
Passage 6:	1a. **B**	1b. **M**	1c. **N**	2. **c**	3. **d**	4. **b**	5. **c**	6. **a**
Passage 7:	1a. **B**	1b. **M**	1c. **N**	2. **b**	3. **c**	4. **b**	5. **d**	6. **a**
Passage 8:	1a. **M**	1b. **B**	1c. **N**	2. **b**	3. **c**	4. **c**	5. **b**	6. **a**
Passage 9:	1a. **N**	1b. **B**	1c. **M**	2. **c**	3. **a**	4. **a**	5. **a**	6. **c**
Passage 10:	1a. **M**	1b. **B**	1c. **N**	2. **d**	3. **d**	4. **b**	5. **c**	6. **c**
Passage 11:	1a. **M**	1b. **B**	1c. **N**	2. **d**	3. **d**	4. **c**	5. **c**	6. **a**
Passage 12:	1a. **M**	1b. **N**	1c. **B**	2. **b**	3. **b**	4. **a**	5. **d**	6. **c**
Passage 13:	1a. **B**	1b. **M**	1c. **N**	2. **b**	3. **c**	4. **a**	5. **b**	6. **c**
Passage 14:	1a. **M**	1b. **N**	1c. **B**	2. **c**	3. **d**	4. **b**	5. **c**	6. **c**
Passage 15:	1a. **M**	1b. **N**	1c. **B**	2. **c**	3. **c**	4. **b**	5. **d**	6. **b**
Passage 16:	1a. **N**	1b. **M**	1c. **B**	2. **b**	3. **d**	4. **d**	5. **c**	6. **c**
Passage 17:	1a. **M**	1b. **N**	1c. **B**	2. **c**	3. **d**	4. **b**	5. **a**	6. **b**
Passage 18:	1a. **N**	1b. **M**	1c. **B**	2. **b**	3. **a**	4. **d**	5. **a**	6. **b**
Passage 19:	1a. **M**	1b. **B**	1c. **N**	2. **b**	3. **c**	4. **d**	5. **c**	6. **d**
Passage 20:	1a. **B**	1b. **M**	1c. **N**	2. **c**	3. **d**	4. **b**	5. **b**	6. **a**

Passage 21:	1a. **M**	1b. **B**	1c. **N**	2. **b**	3. **c**	4. **b**	5. **b**	6. **a**
Passage 22:	1a. **N**	1b. **M**	1c. **B**	2. **b**	3. **c**	4. **b**	5. **a**	6. **b**
Passage 23:	1a. **B**	1b. **M**	1c. **N**	2. **b**	3. **c**	4. **b**	5. **d**	6. **a**
Passage 24:	1a. **N**	1b. **M**	1c. **B**	2. **c**	3. **d**	4. **a**	5. **d**	6. **c**
Passage 25:	1a. **M**	1b. **B**	1c. **N**	2. **d**	3. **b**	4. **c**	5. **c**	6. **b**
Passage 26:	1a. **B**	1b. **N**	1c. **M**	2. **b**	3. **a**	4. **b**	5. **c**	6. **a**
Passage 27:	1a. **B**	1b. **N**	1c. **M**	2. **a**	3. **d**	4. **d**	5. **d**	6. **d**
Passage 28:	1a. **M**	1b. **N**	1c. **B**	2. **c**	3. **d**	4. **b**	5. **c**	6. **a**
Passage 29:	1a. **B**	1b. **N**	1c. **M**	2. **b**	3. **a**	4. **c**	5. **a**	6. **c**
Passage 30:	1a. **B**	1b. **N**	1c. **M**	2. **b**	3. **d**	4. **b**	5. **a**	6. **c**
Passage 31:	1a. **M**	1b. **B**	1c. **N**	2. **d**	3. **b**	4. **b**	5. **b**	6. **b**
Passage 32:	1a. **M**	1b. **B**	1c. **N**	2. **a**	3. **d**	4. **b**	5. **c**	6. **c**
Passage 33:	1a. **M**	1b. **N**	1c. **B**	2. **d**	3. **d**	4. **d**	5. **c**	6. **c**
Passage 34:	1a. **M**	1b. **B**	1c. **N**	2. **d**	3. **a**	4. **a**	5. **b**	6. **b**
Passage 35:	1a. **N**	1b. **M**	1c. **B**	2. **a**	3. **d**	4. **d**	5. **b**	6. **c**
Passage 36:	1a. **M**	1b. **B**	1c. **N**	2. **c**	3. **c**	4. **a**	5. **b**	6. **a**
Passage 37:	1a. **B**	1b. **N**	1c. **M**	2. **c**	3. **b**	4. **c**	5. **a**	6. **c**
Passage 38:	1a. **M**	1b. **N**	1c. **B**	2. **b**	3. **c**	4. **b**	5. **c**	6. **b**
Passage 39:	1a. **M**	1b. **B**	1c. **N**	2. **b**	3. **a**	4. **b**	5. **b**	6. **a**
Passage 40:	1a. **B**	1b. **M**	1c. **N**	2. **d**	3. **d**	4. **a**	5. **b**	6. **d**

Passage 41:	1a. **M**	1b. **B**	1c. **N**	2. **c**	3. **d**	4. **d**	5. **c**	6. **b**
Passage 42:	1a. **N**	1b. **M**	1c. **B**	2. **b**	3. **d**	4. **c**	5. **b**	6. **c**
Passage 43:	1a. **M**	1b. **B**	1c. **N**	2. **b**	3. **a**	4. **c**	5. **d**	6. **b**
Passage 44:	1a. **N**	1b. **B**	1c. **M**	2. **c**	3. **b**	4. **d**	5 .**b**	6. **b**
Passage 45:	1a. **M**	1b. **N**	1c. **B**	2. **c**	3. **c**	4. **d**	5. **b**	6. **c**
Passage 46:	1a. **N**	1b. **B**	1c. **M**	2. **d**	3. **a**	4. **c**	5. **b**	6. **c**
Passage 47:	1a. **B**	1b. **N**	1c. **M**	2. **c**	3. **b**	4. **a**	5. **a**	6. **d**
Passage 48:	1a. **B**	1b. **N**	1c. **M**	2. **d**	3. **c**	4. **b**	5. **a**	6. **d**
Passage 49:	1a. **M**	1b. **B**	1c. **N**	2. **c**	3. **a**	4. **c**	5. **c**	6. **c**
Passage 50:	1a. **B**	1b. **N**	1c. **M**	2. **b**	3. **b**	4. **c**	5. **a**	6. **c**
Passage 51:	1a. **B**	1b. **M**	1c. **N**	2. **c**	3. **b**	4. **d**	5. **c**	6. **a**
Passage 52:	1a. **N**	1b. **B**	1c. **M**	2. **b**	3. **a**	4. **d**	5. **d**	6. **b**
Passage 53:	1a. **N**	1b. **M**	1c. **B**	2. **c**	3. **c**	4. **b**	5. **c**	6. **c**
Passage 54:	1a. **M**	1b. **N**	1c. **B**	2. **c**	3. **d**	4. **d**	5. **d**	6. **a**
Passage 55:	1a. **N**	1b. **M**	1c. **B**	2. **a**	3. **b**	4. **a**	5. **d**	6. **b**
Passage 56:	1a. **M**	1b. **N**	1c. **B**	2. **c**	3. **d**	4. **b**	5. **d**	6. **c**
Passage 57:	1a. **B**	1b. **M**	1c. **N**	2. **b**	3. **d**	4. **b**	5. **b**	6. **a**
Passage 58:	1a. **B**	1b. **N**	1c. **M**	2. **c**	3. **b**	4. **a**	5. **d**	6. **c**
Passage 59:	1a. **N**	1b. **B**	1c. **M**	2. **b**	3. **c**	4. **a**	5. **b**	6. **c**
Passage 60:	1a. **N**	1b. **B**	1c. **M**	2. **c**	3. **b**	4. **c**	5. **d**	6. **a**

Passage 61:	1a. **M**	1b. **N**	1c. **B**	2. **b**	3. **d**	4. **b**	5. **d**	6. **a**
Passage 62:	1a. **M**	1b. **B**	1c. **N**	2. **c**	3. **d**	4. **c**	5. **a**	6. **a**
Passage 63:	1a. **M**	1b. **N**	1c. **B**	2. **a**	3. **b**	4. **c**	5. **b**	6. **a**
Passage 64:	1a. **B**	1b. **N**	1c. **M**	2. **d**	3. **b**	4. **b**	5. **d**	6. **a**
Passage 65:	1a. **M**	1b. **B**	1c. **N**	2. **c**	3. **d**	4. **c**	5. **c**	6. **d**
Passage 66:	1a. **N**	1b. **M**	1c. **B**	2. **d**	3. **a**	4. **c**	5. **a**	6. **d**
Passage 67:	1a. **N**	1b. **B**	1c. **M**	2. **c**	3. **c**	4. **a**	5. **a**	6. **b**
Passage 68:	1a. **N**	1b. **M**	1c. **B**	2. **b**	3. **b**	4. **a**	5. **b**	6. **b**
Passage 69:	1a. **M**	1b. **B**	1c. **N**	2. **c**	3. **c**	4. **a**	5. **d**	6. **d**
Passage 70:	1a. **M**	1b. **B**	1c. **N**	2. **c**	3. **d**	4. **d**	5. **b**	6. **a**
Passage 71:	1a. **M**	1b. **N**	1c. **B**	2. **c**	3. **b**	4. **d**	5. **c**	6. **b**
Passage 72:	1a. **B**	1b. **N**	1c. **M**	2. **d**	3. **b**	4. **d**	5. **b**	6. **c**
Passage 73:	1a. **N**	1b. **M**	1c. **B**	2. **c**	3. **a**	4. **c**	5. **a**	6. **b**
Passage 74:	1a. **M**	1b. **N**	1c. **B**	2. **d**	3. **b**	4. **a**	5. **c**	6. **d**
Passage 75:	1a. **N**	1b. **B**	1c. **M**	2. **d**	3. **d**	4. **c**	5. **b**	6. **c**
Passage 76:	1a. **N**	1b. **B**	1c. **M**	2. **c**	3. **c**	4. **a**	5. **c**	6. **b**
Passage 77:	1a. **B**	1b. **M**	1c. **N**	2. **a**	3. **d**	4. **c**	5. **a**	6. **c**
Passage 78:	1a. **M**	1b. **B**	1c. **N**	2. **d**	3. **c**	4. **b**	5. **a**	6. **a**
Passage 79:	1a. **N**	1b. **M**	1c. **B**	2. **b**	3. **a**	4. **d**	5. **a**	6. **b**
Passage 80:	1a. **M**	1b. **B**	1c. **N**	2. **a**	3. **d**	4. **b**	5. **b**	6. **b**

Passage 81:	1a. **B**	1b. **M**	1c. **N**	2. **a**	3. **d**	4. **a**	5. **b**	6. **c**
Passage 82:	1a. **B**	1b. **M**	1c. **N**	2. **a**	3. **b**	4. **b**	5. **c**	6. **d**
Passage 83:	1a. **B**	1b. **N**	1c. **M**	2. **c**	3. **a**	4. **b**	5. **b**	6. **c**
Passage 84:	1a. **B**	1b. **M**	1c. **N**	2. **c**	3. **b**	4. **a**	5. **a**	6. **d**
Passage 85:	1a. **M**	1b. **N**	1c. **B**	2. **c**	3. **c**	4. **d**	5. **a**	6. **a**
Passage 86:	1a. **B**	1b. **N**	1c. **M**	2. **c**	3. **b**	4. **b**	5. **a**	6. **b**
Passage 87:	1a. **B**	1b. **M**	1c. **N**	2. **a**	3. **d**	4. **c**	5. **a**	6. **a**
Passage 88:	1a. **M**	1b. **N**	1c. **B**	2. **b**	3. **c**	4. **b**	5. **d**	6. **a**
Passage 89:	1a. **N**	1b. **B**	1c. **M**	2. **d**	3. **a**	4. **c**	5. **b**	6. **d**
Passage 90:	1a. **B**	1b. **N**	1c. **M**	2. **b**	3. **a**	4. **c**	5. **c**	6. **d**
Passage 91:	1a. **M**	1b. **B**	1c. **N**	2. **d**	3. **a**	4. **b**	5. **a**	6. **c**
Passage 92:	1a. **M**	1b. **B**	1c. **N**	2. **d**	3. **b**	4. **c**	5. **d**	6. **c**
Passage 93:	1a. **M**	1b. **N**	1c. **B**	2. **c**	3. **c**	4. **d**	5. **a**	6. **c**
Passage 94:	1a. **M**	1b. **N**	1c. **B**	2. **d**	3. **b**	4. **a**	5. **a**	6. **b**
Passage 95:	1a. **B**	1b. **N**	1c. **M**	2. **a**	3. **b**	4. **b**	5. **d**	6. **c**
Passage 96:	1a. **N**	1b. **B**	1c. **M**	2. **c**	3. **b**	4. **c**	5. **c**	6. **b**
Passage 97:	1a. **B**	1b. **N**	1c. **M**	2. **a**	3. **b**	4. **b**	5. **d**	6. **b**
Passage 98:	1a. **M**	1b. **B**	1c. **N**	2. **b**	3. **b**	4. **a**	5. **d**	6. **d**
Passage 99:	1a. **M**	1b. **B**	1c. **N**	2. **b**	3. **c**	4. **d**	5. **c**	6. **d**
Passage 100:	1a. **N**	1b. **B**	1c. **M**	2. **c**	3. **a**	4. **c**	5. **d**	6. **a**

Diagnostic Chart (For Student Correction)

Directions: For each passage, write your answers to the left of the dotted line in the blocks for each skill category. Then correct your answers using the Answer Key on page 203. If your answer is correct, do not make any more marks in the block. If your answer is incorrect, write the letter of the correct answer to the right of the dotted line.

	Categories of Comprehension Skills								
	1 Main Idea			**2**	**3**		**4**	**5**	**6**
	Statement a	Statement b	Statement c	Subject Matter	Supporting Details	Conclusion	Clarifying Devices	Vocabulary in Context	
Passage 1									
Passage 2									
Passage 3									
Passage 4									
Passage 5									
Passage 6									
Passage 7									
Passage 8									
Passage 9									
Passage 10									
Passage 11									
Passage 12									
Passage 13									
Passage 14									
Passage 15									
Passage 16									
Passage 17									
Passage 18									
Passage 19									
Passage 20									

Diagnostic Chart: Passages 21–40

Directions: For each passage, write your answers to the left of the dotted line in the blocks for each skill category. Then correct your answers using the Answer Key on page 204. If your answer is correct, do not make any more marks in the block. If your answer is incorrect, write the letter of the correct answer to the right of the dotted line.

	Categories of Comprehension Skills								
	1 Main Idea				2	3	4	5	6
	Statement a	Statement b	Statement c	Subject Matter	Supporting Details	Conclusion	Clarifying Devices	Vocabulary in Context	
Passage 21									
Passage 22									
Passage 23									
Passage 24									
Passage 25									
Passage 26									
Passage 27									
Passage 28									
Passage 29									
Passage 30									
Passage 31									
Passage 32									
Passage 33									
Passage 34									
Passage 35									
Passage 36									
Passage 37									
Passage 38									
Passage 39									
Passage 40									

Diagnostic Chart: Passages 41–60

Directions: For each passage, write your answers to the left of the dotted line in the blocks for each skill category. Then correct your answers using the Answer Key on page 205. If your answer is correct, do not make any more marks in the block. If your answer is incorrect, write the letter of the correct answer to the right of the dotted line.

	Categories of Comprehension Skills								
	1 Main Idea				2	3	4	5	6
	Statement a	Statement b	Statement c	Subject Matter	Supporting Details	Conclusion	Clarifying Devices	Vocabulary in Context	
Passage 41									
Passage 42									
Passage 43									
Passage 44									
Passage 45									
Passage 46									
Passage 47									
Passage 48									
Passage 49									
Passage 50									
Passage 51									
Passage 52									
Passage 53									
Passage 54									
Passage 55									
Passage 56									
Passage 57									
Passage 58									
Passage 59									
Passage 60									

Diagnostic Chart: Passages 61–80

Directions: For each passage, write your answers to the left of the dotted line in the blocks for each skill category. Then correct your answers using the Answer Key on page 206. If your answer is correct, do not make any more marks in the block. If your answer is incorrect, write the letter of the correct answer to the right of the dotted line.

	Categories of Comprehension Skills								
	1 Main Idea				2	3	4	5	6
	Statement a	Statement b	Statement c	Subject Matter	Supporting Details	Conclusion	Clarifying Devices	Vocabulary in Context	
Passage 61									
Passage 62									
Passage 63									
Passage 64									
Passage 65									
Passage 66									
Passage 67									
Passage 68									
Passage 69									
Passage 70									
Passage 71									
Passage 72									
Passage 73									
Passage 74									
Passage 75									
Passage 76									
Passage 77									
Passage 78									
Passage 79									
Passage 80									

Diagnostic Chart: Passages 81–100

Directions: For each passage, write your answers to the left of the dotted line in the blocks for each skill category. Then correct your answers using the Answer Key on page 207. If your answer is correct, do not make any more marks in the block. If your answer is incorrect, write the letter of the correct answer to the right of the dotted line.

	Categories of Comprehension Skills							
	1 Main Idea			Subject Matter	2 Supporting Details	3 Conclusion	4 Clarifying Devices	5 Vocabulary in Context	6
	Statement a	Statement b	Statement c						
Passage 81									
Passage 82									
Passage 83									
Passage 84									
Passage 85									
Passage 86									
Passage 87									
Passage 88									
Passage 89									
Passage 90									
Passage 91									
Passage 92									
Passage 93									
Passage 94									
Passage 95									
Passage 96									
Passage 97									
Passage 98									
Passage 99									
Passage 100									

Progress Graph

Directions: Write your Total Score for each passage in the comprehension score box under the number of the passage. Then plot your score on the graph itself by putting a small *x* on the line directly above the number of the passage, across from the score you got for that passage. As you mark your score for each passage, graph your progress by drawing a line to connect the *x*'s.

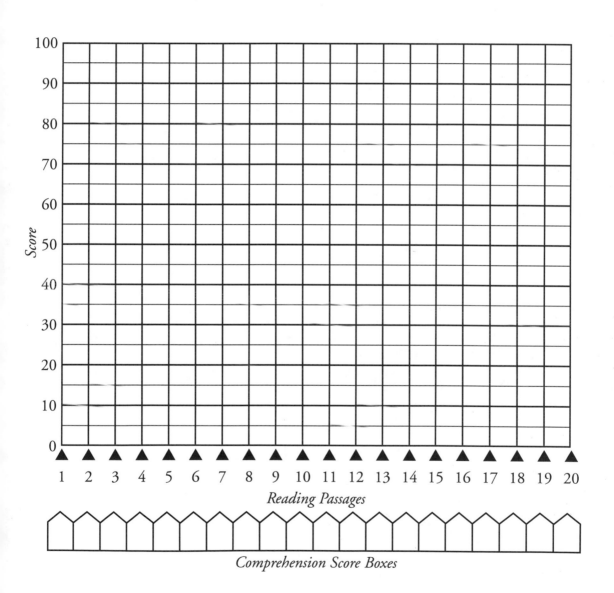

Reading Passages

Comprehension Score Boxes

Progress Graph: Passages 21–40

Directions: Write your Total Score for each passage in the comprehension score box under the number of the passage. Then plot your score on the graph itself by putting a small *x* on the line directly above the number of the passage, across from the score you got for that passage. As you mark your score for each passage, graph your progress by drawing a line to connect the *x*'s.

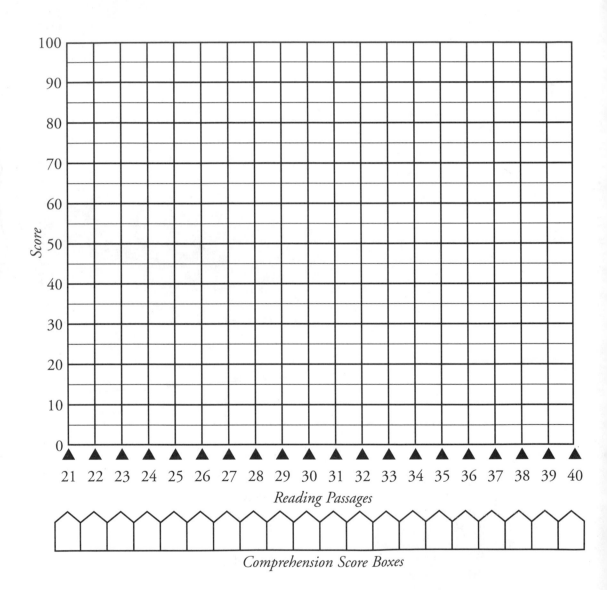

Reading Passages

Comprehension Score Boxes

Progress Graph: Passages 41–60

Directions: Write your Total Score for each passage in the comprehension score box under the number of the passage. Then plot your score on the graph itself by putting a small *x* on the line directly above the number of the passage, across from the score you got for that passage. As you mark your score for each passage, graph your progress by drawing a line to connect the *x*'s.

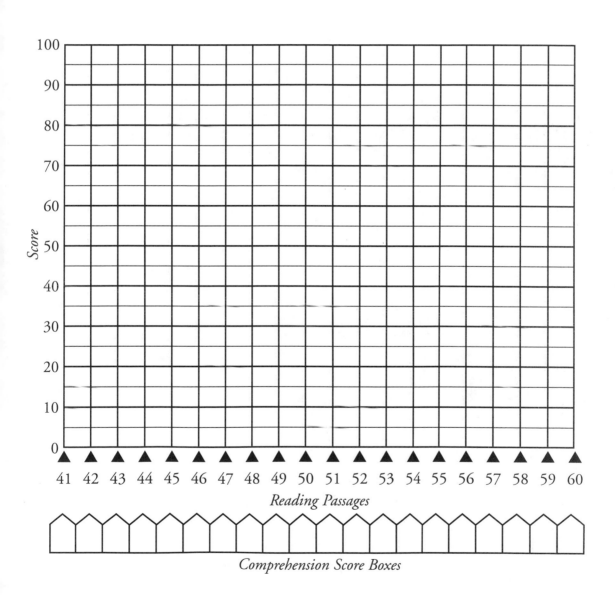

Reading Passages

Comprehension Score Boxes

Progress Graph: Passages 61–80

Directions: Write your Total Score for each passage in the comprehension score box under the number of the passage. Then plot your score on the graph itself by putting a small *x* on the line directly above the number of the passage, across from the score you got for that passage. As you mark your score for each passage, graph your progress by drawing a line to connect the *x*'s.

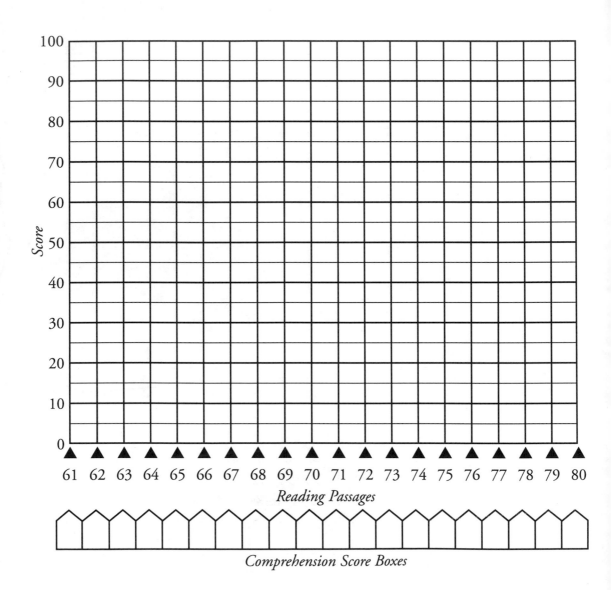

Progress Graph: Passages 81–100

Directions: Write your Total Score for each passage in the comprehension score box under the number of the passage. Then plot your score on the graph itself by putting a small *x* on the line directly above the number of the passage, across from the score you got for that passage. As you mark your score for each passage, graph your progress by drawing a line to connect the *x*'s.

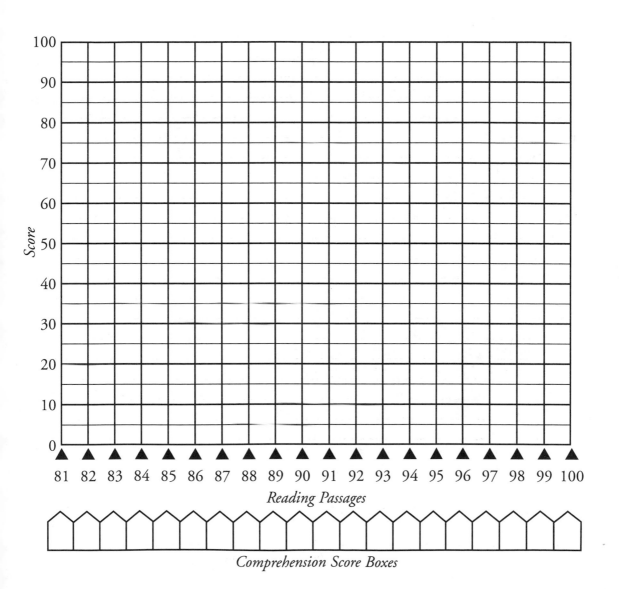

Reading Passages

Comprehension Score Boxes